HANDS-ON HISTORY!
INCAS

STEP INTO THE SPECTACULAR WORLD OF ANCIENT SOUTH AMERICA,
WITH 340 EXCITING PICTURES AND 15 STEP-BY-STEP PROJECTS
PHILIP STEELE   CONSULTANT: DR PENNY DRANSART

ARMADILLO

This edition is published by Armadillo
an imprint of Anness Publishing Ltd
info@anness.com
www.annesspublishing.com

If you like the images in this book and would
like to investigate using them for publishing,
promotions or advertising, please visit our website
www.practicalpictures.com for more information.

© Anness Publishing Ltd 2013

Publisher: Joanna Lorenz
Managing Editor: Gilly Cameron Cooper
Project Editor: Joy Wotton
Editor: Nicola Baxter
Designer: Margaret Sadler
Illustrations: Rob Ashby, Vanessa Card, Clive Spong
Project Photography: John Freeman
Stylist: Melanie Williams
Production Controller: Yolande Denny

PUBLISHER'S NOTE
Although the advice and information in this book are
believed to be accurate and true at the time of going to
press, neither the authors nor the publisher can accept any
legal responsibility or liability for any errors or omissions
that may have been made nor for any inaccuracies nor for
any loss, harm or injury that comes about from following
instructions or advice in this book.

PICTURE CREDITS
(b=bottom, t=top, m=middle, l=left, r=right)
AKG: pages 9ml, 9r, 11tl, 12t, 15m, 41bl, 60b; The
Ancient Art and Architecture Collection Ltd: pages 4l, 10l,
11ml, 21t, 51tl, 57tl; Andes Press Agency: pages 15t, 20t,
40tr, 45b, 53bl; The Bridgeman Art Library: page 40ml;
Jean-Loup Charmet: pages 53t, 53br; Bruce Coleman:
pages 19ml, 42br, 49br; Sue Cunningham Photographic:
pages 2bl, 5tr, 16t, 18l, 19tl, 23tl, 23tr, 24t, 31bl, 46t,
50m, 56ml, 56m, 58tr, 60mr; E.T. Archive: pages 3tr, 8r,
26t, 26mr, 27bl, 35m, 37tl, 37ml, 39m, 42ml, 54bl, 58tl,
60tl; Mary Evans Picture Library: pages 9tl, 9m, 61b;
Werner Forman Archive: pages 2t, 2br, 3br, 4mr, 10r, 14l,
14r, 17t, 27tl, 31tr, 32t, 33ml, 33tr, 34ml, 35tr, 36mr,
38l, 46m, 47m, 48t, 51bl, 52t, 52br, 59ml; Michael
Holford: pages 29b, 34t, 38mr, 57tr; The Hutchison
Library: endpapers, pages 20bl, 20r, 28t, 47t; Chris
Kapolka: page 44bl; Panos: page 16r, 55b; Planet Earth:
page 22b; Popperfoto: page 43tr; N.J. Saunders: page 13b;
Science Photo Library: pages 35tl, 39ml, 49l, 49ml; South
American Pictures: pages 1, 5mr, 8l, 11tr, 13t, 13m, 15bl,
16bl, 17r, 17bl, 17r, 18r, 19r, 21br, 22t, 24l, 24b, 25t,
25bl, 26m, 28bl, 28br, 29t, 30l, 30r, 32l, 36l,
41tl, 41tr, 42tr, 43tl, 43bl, 44t, 44br, 45t,
45m, 48bl, 48br, 49tr, 50t, 52bl, 54t, 54br,
55t, 55m, 57ml, 58m, 59t, 61tl, 61tr; Still
Pictures: pages 5tl, 12b, 39tr, 40mr, 51tl;
Wilderness Photo Library: page 4tr.

CONTENTS

Manufacturer: Anness Publishing Ltd, Blaby Road,
Wigston, Leicestershire LE18 4SE, England
For Product Tracking go to:
www.annesspublishing.com/tracking
Batch: 1443-22315-1127

Anness Publishing would like to thank the following children for appearing in this book: Jake Lewis, Courtney Andrews, Sabirah Bari, Patrick Clifford, Molly Cooper, Daniel Djanan, Jodie King, Graham Oppong, Joshua Adam Laidlaw Parkin, Adrianne S. Punzalan, Katie Louise Stevens, Samantha Street, Reece Warman.

Peoples of the Andes

Snowy peaks and glaciers rim the skyline above high, open plateaus. Cold lakes reflect the blue sky. These are the South American Andes, stretching for about 7,600km/ 4,700 miles from Colombia to southern Chile. To the west, plains and deserts border the Pacific Ocean. To the east, steamy rainforests surround the Amazon River.

Humans settled here in about 11,000BC, or even earlier. Their ancestors crossed into North America from Asia and moved south. As the climate became warmer, tribes settled in the Andes and on the coast. They learned to farm and build villages. From about 1000BC, the seven civilizations of the Parácas, Chavín, Nazca, Moche, Tiwanaku, Wari and Chimú rose and fell. Last of all, from around AD1100 to 1532, came the Inca Empire.

IN THE HIGH ANDES
Alpacas cross a snowfield, high in the Andes. These woolly animals are related to the South American llama, guanaco and vicuña. Their wild ancestors may have been tamed in the Andes as early as 5400BC. Herding and farming were not essential for allowing great civilizations in the Andes, but the Incas developed these activities with great skill.

WORKERS OF GOLD
Hollow golden hands from a Chimú tomb may have been used as incense holders. The Chimú people came to power in northern Peru about 400 years before the Incas. Their smiths became very skilled at working gold. These craftsmen were later employed by the Incas.

DIGGING UP THE PAST
Archaeologists work near Sipán, in Peru's Lambayeque Valley. Burials of a warrior-priest and of Moche royalty, dating from about AD300, have been found there. The ancient Andean peoples kept no written records, so all we know of them comes from archaeology.

TIMELINE 11,000BC–AD1

Thousands of years before the Inca Empire was founded, people had settled on the Peruvian coast and in the Andes. The ruins of their cities and temples still stood in Inca times. They were part of the Inca world.

c.11,000BC People settle at Monte Verde, Chile.

c.10,000BC Stone tools are in use in Peru.

c.9000BC The climate becomes warmer, and glaciers retreat.

c.8600BC Beans, bottle gourds and chilli peppers are cultivated.

c.7500BC Guanaco, vicuña and deer become common in the Andes and are hunted for food.

c.5400BC Alpacas, and probably llamas, are herded.

Farming spreads along the coast and in the highlands.

c.4500BC Andean farmers cultivate squash.

stone tools

c.3800BC Maize, manioc and cotton are grown in the Andes.

c.3500BC Llamas are used as pack animals to transport goods.

llama

c.3200–1500BC Mummification is used to preserve the bodies of dead people in the north of Chile.

c.2800BC Pottery is made in Ecuador and in Colombia.

c.2600BC Temples are built on platform mounds on the Peruvian coast.

11,000BC   8600BC   3800BC   2500BC

NAZCA PUZZLES

Mysterious markings on the ground were scraped on the desert on a gigantic scale by the Nazca people. Their civilization grew up on the coast of southern Peru, a thousand years before the Incas. The lines may have marked out routes for religious processions.

VALLEY OF MYSTERY

The Urubamba River winds through steep, forested gorges. In 1911, an American archaeologist called Dr Hiram Bingham came to the area in search of Inca ruins. He discovered a lost city on the slopes of Machu Picchu, high above the river valley.

ANCIENT PEOPLES

This man is one of the Aymara people who live around Lake Titicaca, on the high border between Peru and Bolivia. Some historians believe they are descended from the builders of a great city called Tiwanaku. Others say that they arrived from the Cañete Valley after Tiwanaku was abandoned in about 1250. Although their way of life has changed over the ages, the Aymara have kept a distinctive identity.

IN SOUTH AMERICA

The great civilizations of South America grew up in the far west of the continent. The area is now occupied by the modern countries of Colombia, Ecuador, Peru, Bolivia, Chile and Argentina.

*c.*2500BC A temple with stepped platforms is built at El Paraíso on the coast of Peru.

Backstrap looms are used.

backstrap loom

Potatoes and *quinua* are cultivated.

There is widespread fishing along the Peruvian coast and the northern coast of Chile.

quinua Andean farmers use irrigation.

*c.*2000BC The farming of maize, which first developed on the south-central coast and the north coast, is now widespread along the Peruvian coast and in the highlands.

*c.*1800BC Pottery-making develops along the coast of Peru.

*c.*1500BC Metal-working develops in Peru.

*c.*1000BC Large-scale settlement takes place in the Andes.

*c.*900BC The Chavín culture develops. The temple complex at Chavín de Huantar is built.

*c.*700BC The Parácas culture begins to thrive.

*c.*200BC The Chavín culture comes to an end.

The Nazca culture develops on the coast of southern Peru. Gigantic Nazca lines are marked on the surface of the deserts.

Chavín stone head

2000BC

900BC

AD1

The Great Empire

WHO WERE THE INCAS and where did they come from? If you had asked them, they would have told you proudly that their first great ruler, Manko Qapaq, was sent to Earth by his father Inti, the Sun. Manko Qapaq's queen, Mama Okllo, was believed to be the daughter of the Moon.

The Incas believed that they were superior to all other peoples. In reality, they were just the last link in a long chain of civilizations. They shared many beliefs with these peoples, often taking over their technology and crafts. From their mountain homeland, they learned how to live in the same landscapes and make use of them, ruling coast, desert and rainforest. The Incas started out as just one of many small tribes living in the Peruvian Andes in the 1100s. In the 1300s, led by their ruler Mayta Qapaq, they began to conquer nearby lands. During the 1400s, Inca armies and officials created a huge Empire. Although the Incas themselves only numbered about 40,000, they ruled a total population of about 12 million. Of the 20 languages that were spoken in the Inca Empire, the most important was Quechua, which is still widely spoken in the Andes mountains today.

This vast Empire seemed as if it would last for ever. In 1532, something happened to change that. Spanish soldiers landed in Peru, greedy for gold and land.

TAWANTINSUYU
The Incas called their Empire Tawantinsuyu (the Four Quarters). This name referred to the regions of Chinchaysuyu, Collasuyu, Antisuyu and Cuntisuyu (North, South, East and West). Their borders met at Cuzco, the capital, known as the "navel of the world". At the height of its power, during the 1400s, Tawantinsuyu stretched 3,600km/2,250 miles from north to south, and about 320km/200 miles inland across the Andes. This immense Empire took in the lands that now make up Peru, northern Chile, the far west of Argentina, part of Bolivia, Ecuador and the southern borders of Colombia.

Moche stirrup spout f...

Timeline AD1–1492

*C.*AD1 The Moche culture begins to thrive.

The Moche culture produces skilled goldsmiths and potters.

*C.*AD100 The great city-state of Tiwanaku grows up near Lake Titicaca in southern Peru.

Moche ceramic pot of a barn owl

*C.*AD200 The Parácas culture declines.

AD500 Tiwanaku is now a major city of 40,000 to 100,000 inhabitants.

*C.*AD600 The Gateway of the Sun is built at the city of Tiwanaku.

Gateway of the Sun

*C.*AD700 The Moche culture in the north comes to an end.

Wari city-state is at its height.

The Chimú culture, based at Chan Chan, begins to thrive.

*C.*AD750 The Nazca culture comes to an end.

*C.*AD900 Chimú becomes a major power.

AD1000 Wari city-state is abandoned.

*C.*1100 Manko Qapaq, the legendary first Inca emperor, founds Cuzco.

Wari winged figure

AD1   AD500   AD750   AD1250

Spanish soldier

QUITO

ANDES MOUNTAINS

Amazon River

TUMBES

sun god mask

CAJAMARCA
CHAN CHAN
MOCHE

macaw

CHAVIN DE HUANTAR

alpaca

panpipes

MACHU PICCHU
PISAQ
CUZCO

PARACAS
NAZCA

Inca warrior

LAKE TITICACA

Nazca hummingbird figure

reed boat

TIWANAKU

guinea pig

c.1250 The once-great city of Tiwanaku is abandoned, perhaps because of changes in the climate.

c.1300 Sinchi Roka is the first emperor to use the title *Sapa Inca*.

1370 Chimor, the Empire of the Chimú people, expands.

c.1410 The Incas make new alliances under the emperor Wiraqocha.

1437 Wiraqocha's son Yupanki conquers the mountain State of Chanca.

Chimú gold funeral mask

1438 Wiraqocha backs another son, Urqon, as the next emperor.

Yupanki proclaims himself emperor of a rival Inca State and renames himself Pachakuti.

Urqon is killed, and his father Wiraqocha dies.

The Inca State is reunited under Pachakuti.

c.1440 The powerful emperor, Minchançaman, rules Chimú.

c.1445 Pachakuti's brother, Qapaq Yupanki, explores the coastline to the south.

c.1450 Incas build Machu Picchu high in the Andes.

1450 The Inca Empire grows by conquest. Cuzco is rebuilt.

1470 Incas conquer Chimor.

1471 Topa Inka Yupanki becomes emperor. A great age of road building begins.

Chimú ritual knife

AD1438

AD1445

AD1492

Makers of History

BECAUSE INCA HISTORY was not written down at the time, much of it has to be pieced together from chronicles and diaries recorded in the years after the Spanish conquest in the 1500s. Many accounts describe the everyday lives of ordinary people in the days of the Inca Empire. The names of the people who dug the fields and built the roads are mostly forgotten. Only the names of the Inca royal family and the nobles are known.

The first eight emperors recalled in Inca folklore probably did exist. However, over the centuries, their life stories, passed on from parent to child over generations, became mixed up with

myths and legends. The last 100 years of Inca rule, beginning when Pachakuti Inka Yupanki came to the throne in 1438, were fresh in people's memories when the Spanish invaded.

As a result, we know a good deal about the greatest days of the Inca Empire.

MAMA OKLLO
This painting from the 1700s imagines the Inca empress, Mama Okllo, carrying a Moon mask. She reigned in the 1100s. In some Inca myths, she and her brother Manko Qapaq were said to be the children of the Sun and the Moon. Mama Okllo married her brother, who became the first ruler of the Incas. They had a son called Sinchi Roka.

ON THE ROAD TO RUIN
An Inca emperor and empress are carried around their Empire. The Inca rulers had almost unlimited power, but were destroyed by bitter rivalry within the royal family. When the Spanish invaders arrived in 1532, Tawantinsuyu was divided between supporters of Waskar and his brother Ataw Wallpa.

TIMELINE AD1492–1781

1492 The Incas conquer northern Chile.

1493 Wayna Qapaq becomes emperor.

1498 Wayna Qapaq conquers part of Colombia and the Inca Empire reaches its greatest extent.

c.1523 A ship-wrecked Spaniard called Alejo García enters Inca territory from the east with raiding Chiriquana warriors. He dies during his return journey.

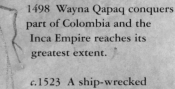

quipu used for government records

1525 Wayna Qapaq dies without an agreed successor. His son Waskar is chosen and crowned as the twelfth *Sapa Inca* in Cuzco. Waskar's brother, Ataw Wallpa, claims the imperial throne.

War breaks out in the Inca Empire as the brothers battle for power.

1526–7 A Spanish naval expedition sights Inca rafts off the Pacific coast.

Inca warrior

1529 The Spanish king approves a plan by Francisco Pizarro to conquer Peru.

1532 Waskar is defeated by his brother Ataw Wallpa.

The Spanish, under Francisco Pizarro, enter the inland city of Cajamarca and kill 7,000 Incas.

1533 Ataw Wallpa and his sister, Asarpay, are killed by the Spanish.

Inca rope bridge

AD1492   AD1525   AD1529   AD1535

8

LLOQE YUPANKI

The son of Sinchi Roka, Lloqe Yupanki was chosen to be ruler of the lands around Cuzco in place of his older brother. He was a wise ruler, and his reign in the 1200s was peaceful. His son Mayta Qapaq was more warlike. He expanded his Empire by conquering other peoples.

PACHAKUTI INKA YUPANKI (REIGNED 1438–71)

Inka Yupanki was still a prince when he proved himself in war by conquering the Chanca people. However, his father Wiraqocha chose another son, Inka Urqon, as the next emperor. Yupanki claimed the throne, calling himself Pachakuti, which means 'the world turned upside down'. Urqon was killed, and his father died soon after.

ATAW WALLPA (REIGNED 1532–3)

Known as Atahuallpa or Atabaliba to the Spanish, Ataw Wallpa was the son of the great emperor Wayna Qapaq, who died unexpectedly in 1525. When his brother Waskar was crowned in Cuzco, Ataw Wallpa stayed with the army in the north, and a bitter war followed. By 1532, Waskar had been imprisoned, and Ataw Wallpa was ruler. But before the Empire could recover from the war, the Spanish invaded. Ataw Wallpa was captured and executed the following summer.

FRANCISCO PIZARRO (c.1478–1541)

In 1532, this Spanish soldier sailed to the Inca city of Tumbes with just 180 men and 37 horses. They marched inland to Cajamarca. Pizarro used treachery to capture and kill the Inca emperor, Ataw Wallpa. This army went on to loot Inca gold and bring Peru under Spanish rule. Resistance from the local people was fierce – but not as fierce as the rivalry and greed of the Spanish. Pizarro was murdered by one of his fellow countrymen fewer than ten years later.

1535 The Incas rebel against Spain.

1536 Incas lay siege to the city of Cuzco. The city is burned to the ground by the Incas.

The Inca Empire collapses.

1537 A last Inca State is formed by Cura Okllo and Manko Inka, based at Vilcabamba.

1538 The Spanish invaders fight among themselves at Las Salinas, near Cuzco.

Inca messenger with conch shell

1539 Cura Okllo, the successor to Asarpay and the sister-wife of Manko Inka, is executed by the Spanish.

1541 Pizarro is assassinated.

1545 Manko Inka is assassinated.

1572 Inca resistance under Tupac Amaru I is finally defeated, and he is executed. He is the last Inca ruler.

Vilcabamba and Machu Picchu are abandoned.

1742 Resistance to the Spanish grows. Calls for restoration of the Inca Empire.

1780 Major uprising of indigenous peoples under José Gabriel Condorcanqui He adopts the name of his ancestor and declares himself Tupac Amaru II. He aims to restore the Inca Empire.

1781 Tupac Amaru II is captured and horribly tortured to death.

Spanish conquistador

AD1539   AD1742   AD1781

Lords of the Sun

MANY OF THE EARLY TRIBES that lived in the Andes and on the Pacific coast were small groups of hunters and farmers. As cities and kingdoms grew in size, they began to need strong leadership. By about AD900, the State of Chimor was headed by powerful kings.

The Inca emperor was called *Sapa Inca* (Only Leader). As a descendant of the Sun, he was regarded as a god. He had complete power over his subjects, but he always had to be on his guard. There were many rivals for the throne among his royal relations. Each emperor had a new palace built for himself in the royal city of Cuzco. Emperors were treated with the utmost respect at all times and were often veiled or screened from ordinary people.

The empress, or *Quya* (Star), was the emperor's sister or mother. She was also thought to be divine and led the worship of the Moon goddess. The next

emperor was supposed to be chosen from among her sons. An emperor had many secondary wives. Waskar was said to have fathered eighty children in just eight years.

RELIGIOUS LEADERS
Sacrifices of llamas were made to the gods each month, at special festivals and before battle. The *Sapa Inca* controlled all religious activities. In the 1400s, the emperor Wiraqocha Inka declared that worship of the god Wiraqocha, the Creator (after whom he was named), was more important than worship of Inti, the Sun god. This made some people angry.

A CHOSEN WOMAN
Young girls, the *akllakuna*, were educated for four years in religious matters, weaving and housekeeping. Some became the emperor's secondary wives or married noblemen. Others became priestesses or *mamakuna* (virgins of the Sun). Figurines like these wore specially made clothes, but these have perished or been lost over the years.

A FEATHER FAN
You will need: pencil, thin card, ruler, scissors, bright paints, paintbrush, water pot, masking tape, padding, white glue, sackcloth, needle, thread, string or twine.

1 Draw a feather shape 18cm/7in long on to card and cut it out. The narrow part should be half of this length. Draw around the shape on card nine times.

2 Carefully paint the card feathers brightly. Use red, orange and yellow paints to look like rainforest birds. Allow the paint to dry completely.

3 Cut out each feather and snip along the sides of the widest part to give a feathery effect. When the paint is dry, paint the other side as well.

COMMANDER IN CHIEF

The emperor sits on his throne. He wears a tasselled wool headdress or *llautu*, decorated with gold and feathers, and large gold earplugs. He carries a sceptre. Around him, army chiefs await their orders. Emperors played an active part in military campaigns and relied on the army to keep them in power.

COOL SPRINGS

At Tambo Machay, to the south of Cuzco, fresh, cold water flows in from sacred springs. Here, the great Pachakuti Inka Yupanki would bathe after a hard day's hunting.

THE LIVING DEAD

The dead body of an emperor, preserved as a mummy, is paraded through the streets. When each emperor died, his palace became his tomb. Once a year, the body was carried around Cuzco amid great celebrations. The picture is by Guamán Poma de Ayala, who was of Inca descent. In the 1600s, he made many pictures of Inca life.

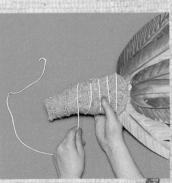

Feathers from birds of the tropical forests to the east of the Andes were used to make fans for the emperor.

4 Hold the narrow ends of the feathers and spread out the tops to form a fan shape. Use masking tape to secure the ends firmly in position.

5 Cut a piece of padding 9cm/3½in high and long enough to wrap the base of the feathers several times. Use glue on one side to keep it in place.

6 Cut a strip of sackcloth about 5cm/2in wide. Starting at the base of the feathers, wrap the fabric around the stems. Hold it in place with a few stitches.

7 Wind string or twine firmly around the sackcloth to form the fan's handle. Tuck in the ends and use glue at each end to make sure they are secure.

The Inca State

AMILY CONNECTIONS PLAYED an important part in royal power struggles and in everyday social organization in the Inca world. The nobles were grouped into family-based corporations called *panakas*. Members of each *panaka* shared rights to an area of land, its water, pasture and herds. Linked to each *panaka* was a land-holding *ayllu* (or clan) – a group of common people who were also related to each other.

The Incas managed to control an empire that contained many different peoples. Loyal Incas were sent to live in remote areas, while troublemakers from the regions were resettled nearer Cuzco, where they could be carefully watched. Conquered chiefs were called *kurakas*. They and their children were educated in Inca ways and allowed to keep some of their local powers.

The Inca system of law was quite severe. State officials and *kurakas* (conquered chiefs) acted as judges. Those who stole from the emperor's stores of grain, textiles and other goods faced a death sentence. Torture, beating, blinding and exile were all common punishments. The age of the criminal and the reason for the crime were sometimes taken into account.

A CLEVER CALCULATOR

One secret of Inca success was the *quipu*. It was used by government officials for recording all kinds of information, from the number of households in a town to the amount of goods of various kinds in a warehouse. The *quipu* was a series of strings tied to a thick cord. Each string had one or more colours and could be knotted. The colours represented anything from types of grain to groups of people. The knots represented numbers.

ONE STATE, MANY PEOPLES

The ancestors of these Bolivian women were subjects of the Incas. The Inca Empire was the largest ever known in all the Americas. It included at least a hundred different peoples. The Incas were clever governors and did not always try to force their own ideas upon other groups. Conquered peoples had to accept the Inca gods, but they were allowed to worship in their own way and keep their own customs.

A ROYAL INSPECTION

Topa Inka Yupanki inspects government stores in the 1470s. In the Inca world, nearly all grain, textiles and other goods were produced for the State and stored in warehouses. Some extra produce might be bartered, or exchanged privately, but there were no big markets or stores.

PUBLIC WORKS

Workers build fortifications on the borders of the Inca Empire. People paid their taxes to the Inca State in the form of work called *mit'a*. This might be general work on the land. Men were also conscripted to work on public buildings or serve in the army. The Spanish continued to operate the *mit'a* as a form of tax long after they conquered the Inca Empire.

OLLANTAYTAMBO

This building in Ollantaytambo, in the Urubamba Valley, was once a State storehouse for the farm produce of the region. Ollantaytambo was a large town, which was probably built about 550 years ago. It protected the valley from raids by the warriors who lived in the forests to the east. Buildings dating from the Inca Empire were still being lived in by local people when the American archaeologist Dr Hiram Bingham passed through in 1911.

Nobles and Peasants

INCA SOCIETY was strictly graded. At the top were the *Sapa Inca* and his *Quya*. The High Priest and other important officials were normally recruited from members of the royal family.

If noblemen were loyal to the emperor, they might receive gifts of land. They might be given gold or a beautiful *akllakuna* as a wife. They could expect jobs as regional governors, generals or priests. Lords and ladies wore fine clothes and were carried in splendid chairs, called litters.

Next in rank were the conquered non-Inca rulers and chiefs, the *kurakas*. They were cleverly brought into the Inca political system and given traditional distinctions. They served as regional judges.

Most people in the Empire were peasants. They were unable to leave their villages without official permission. They had no choice but to stay and toil on the land, sending their produce to the government stores.

CRAFT AND CLASS
A pottery figure from the Peruvian coast shows a porter carrying a water pot on his back. In the Inca Empire, craft workers such as potters and goldsmiths were employed by the State. They formed a small middle class. Unlike peasants they were never made to do *mit'a* (public service).

A MOCHE NOBLEMAN
The man's face on this jar is that of a noble. It was made by a Moche potter on the north coast of Peru between 1,500 and 2,000 years ago. The man's headdress sets him apart as a noble, perhaps a high priest.

A WATER POT
You will need: self-drying clay, cutting board, rolling pin, ruler, water, water pot, acrylic paints, paintbrush.

1 Roll out a piece of clay on the board. Make a circle about 17cm/6¾in in diameter and 1cm/½in thick. This will form the base of your water pot.

2 Roll some more clay into long sausages, about as fat as your little finger. Dampen the base with water and carefully place a sausage around the edge.

3 Coil more clay sausages on top of each other to build up the pot. Make each coil slightly smaller than the one below. Water will help them stick.

A Peasant's Life

A woman harvests potatoes near Sicuani, to the south of Cuzco. Then, as now, life was hard for the peasant farmers of the Andes. Both men and women worked in the fields, and even young children and the elderly were expected to help. However, the Inca State did provide some support for the peasants, supplying free grain in times of famine.

Plugged In

This Chimú earplug is made of gold, turquoise and shell. It was worn as a badge of rank. Inca noblemen wore such heavy gold earplugs that the Spanish called them *orejones* (big ears). Noblewomen wore their hair long, covered with a head-cloth.

Land and Seasons

One third of all land and produce belonged to the emperor, one third to the priests and one third to the peasants. It was hardly a fair division. A peasant's life, digging, planting and harvesting, was ruled by the seasons. Each new season was celebrated by religious festivals and ceremonies.

Children were expected to help their parents by fetching water from the wells and mountain springs.

4 When you reach the neck of the pot, start making the coils slightly bigger again to form a lip. Carefully smooth the coils with wet fingertips.

5 Use two more rolls of clay to make handles on opposite sides of the pot. Smooth out the joints carefully to make sure the handles stay in place.

6 Leave the clay to dry completely. Then paint the pot all over with a background shade. Choose an earthy reddish brown to look like Inca pottery.

7 Leave the reddish brown paint to dry. Use a fine paintbrush and black paint to draw Inca designs on the pot like the ones in the picture above.

15

On Land and Water

PERU TODAY is still criss-crossed by the remains of cobbled roads built by the Incas. Two main paved highways ran north to south, one following the coast and the other following the Andes. The first was about 3,600km/2,235 miles long, the second even longer.

The two roads were joined by smaller roads linking towns and villages. The roads crossed deserts, mountains and plateaus. Markers measured out distances in *topos*, units of about 7km/4 miles.

Despite these great engineering works, most people in the Empire were not allowed to travel at all. These fine roads were strictly for use by people on official business. Messages to and from the emperor were carried by trained relay runners called *chasquis*, who were stationed in stone shelters along the way. In one day, a message could travel 240km/150 miles. Government rest-houses called *tambos* were built on the chief routes.

The Incas were very inventive, but they had no wheeled transport. Baggage and goods were carried by porters or on the backs of llamas. Nobles journeyed in richly decorated litters, carried by four or more men.

THE WATER CARRIER
A porter carries a jar on his head. Steep mountain roads must have made such work very tiring. The State road network allowed crops, food, drink, precious metal ores and textiles to be brought to the royal court from far-flung regions of the Empire.

GOING TO WAR
A litter, carried at shoulder height by four strong men, carries the emperor Wayna Qapaq to war. One purpose of the Inca road network was to make sure that armies could be moved quickly from one end of the Empire to the other. Depots and food stores for army use were built along the highways. Depot managers were kept in a state of readiness by royal officials.

THE ROAD GOES ON
An old Inca road zigzags up steep, terraced slopes near Pisaq. Inca engineers laid down about 16,000km/10,000 miles of roads in all. Some highway sections were up to 7m/7yds across. Most were just broad enough for a llama – about 1m/1yd wide. The steepest sections were stepped.

BOATS OF REEDS

These modern boats were made by the Uru people of Lake Titicaca. The Incas made boats and rafts for travel on lakes, rivers and the ocean. Because there was a shortage of timber in most areas, they made them from a type of reed, called *totora*. These were cut, trimmed and tightly bound in bundles. They were light, buoyant and strong, and could be bent into curved shapes to form the prow and stern of a boat.

HIGHWAY PATROL

The governor of bridges watches as a porter carrying goods on his back crosses a rope bridge across a mountain river. Bridges had to be able to take considerable stress and strain, caused by the tramp of marching armies and by hundreds of heavily burdened llamas. Officials inspected roads and bridges and could order local workers to repair them under the *mit'a* system of conscripted work.

BRIDGES OF ROPE

Rope bridges are still made from woven mountain grasses by the Quechua people. This one crosses a gorge of the Apurimac River in Peru. Inca engineers built long rope bridges like this one, as well as stone bridges, causeways over marshy ground and tunnels through rock. Sometimes people crossed rivers in baskets hauled across the water on ropes.

Master Masons

THE ROCKS of the Andes mountains provided high quality granite that was used for impressive public buildings. These included temples, fortresses, palaces, holy shrines and aqueducts (stone channels for carrying water supplies).

The *mit'a* work system provided the workforce. In the quarries, massive rocks weighing up to 120 tons were cracked and shifted with stone hammers and bronze crowbars. They were hauled with ropes on log rollers or sleds. On site, the stones were shaped to fit and rubbed smooth with water and sand. Smaller stone blocks were used for upper walls or lesser buildings.

The expert Inca stonemasons had only basic tools. They used plumblines (weighted cords) to make sure that walls were straight. They used no mortar or cement, but the stones fitted together perfectly. Many remain in place to this day. Most public buildings were on a grand scale, but all were of a simple design.

BRINGER OF WATER
This beautifully engineered stone water-channel was built across a valley floor by Inca stonemasons. Aqueducts, often covered, were used both for irrigation and for drinking supplies. Irrigation schemes were being built in Peru as early as around 4,500 years ago.

BUILDING THE TEMPLE
These rectangular stone blocks were part of the holiest site in the Inca Empire, the *Coricancha* (Temple of the Sun). Inca stonework was deliberately designed to withstand the earthquakes that regularly shake the region. The original temple on this site was badly damaged by a tremor in 1650.

AN INCA GRANARY
You will need: ruler, pencil, beige, dark and cream thin card, scissors, white pencil, paints, paintbrush, water container, pair of compasses, masking tape, white glue, hay or straw.

1 Use a ruler and pencil to mark eight strips 8.5cm/ 3½in long and 3mm/⅛in wide, and one strip 36cm/ 14½in long and 3mm/⅛in wide on beige card. Cut out.

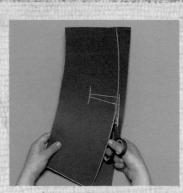

2 On the dark card, draw a curved shape 34cm/ 13½in along the base, 11cm/ 4½in in height and 30cm/12in along the top. Cut out. Cut a doorway 6cm/2½in high.

3 Paint another piece of card to look like stone. Let it dry. Cut it into 'blocks' 2cm/¾in high. Glue them one by one on to the building shape.

HISTORY IN STONE

Stone walls and streets, such as these fine examples still standing in Ollantaytambo, survive to tell a story. Archaeology is much more difficult in the rainforests to the east, where timber structures rot rapidly in the hot, moist air. That is one reason we know more about the way people lived in the Andes than in the Amazon region.

INCA DESIGN

A building in Machu Picchu shows an example of typical Inca design. Inca stonemasons learned many of their skills from earlier Peruvian civilizations. Openings that are wider at the bottom than the top are seen only in Inca buildings. They are said to be trapezoid.

A MASSIVE FORTRESS

Llamas still pass before the mighty walls of Sacsahuaman, at Cuzco. This building was a fortress with towers and terraces. It also served as a royal palace and a sacred shrine. Its multi-sided boulders are precisely fitted. It is said to have been built over many years by 30,000 workers. It was one of many public buildings raised in the reign of Pachakuti Inka Yupanki.

Storehouses were built of neat stone blocks. They kept precious grain dry and secure.

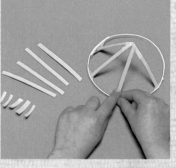

4 Use the compasses to draw a circle 18cm/7in across on cream card. Cut out and cut off one quarter. Tape the straight cut edges together to form a cone.

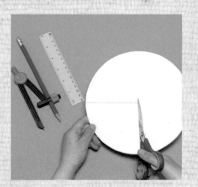

5 Make a circle by joining the ends of the 36cm/ 14½in strip with tape. Attach the 8.5cm/3½in long strips around the edge and in the middle as shown.

6 Glue short lengths of straw or hay all over the card cone to form the thatched roof of the granary. The thatch should all run in the same direction.

7 Attach the edges of the walls with masking tape. Fold in the sides of the doorway. Place the rafters on top. The thatched roof fits on the rafters.

Town Dwellers

REAT CITIES had been built in Peru long before the Incas came to power. In about AD600, the city of Tiwanaku, near Lake Titicaca, may have had a population of nearly 100,000. A hundred years later, the Chimú capital of Chan Chan covered 15 square kilometres/9½ square miles of the coastal plain.

The Inca capital, Cuzco, was ringed by mountains and crossed by two rivers that had been turned into canals, the Huatanay and the Tullamayo. Cuzco became dominated by fine public buildings and royal palaces when it was rebuilt in about 1450. At its heart was the great public square, known as *Waqaypata* (Holy Place). At festival time, this square was packed with crowds. Roads passed from here to the four quarters of the empire. They were lined by the homes of Inca nobles, facing in upon private compounds called *canchas*. The middle of the city was home to about 40,000 people, but the surrounding suburbs and villages housed another 200,000. Newer Inca towns, such as Pumpo, Huanuco and Tambo Colorado, were planned in much the same way as Cuzco, but adapted to the local landscape.

WATER ON TAP
At Machu Picchu, water was brought into the town from the mountain springs that bubbled up about 1.5km/1 mile outside the city walls. The water ran into stone troughs and fountains, and it was used for bathing and drinking.

THE PAST REVEALED
Archaeologists record every detail of what they find with the greatest care. Here at an old Inca town near Cuzco, they are using precision instruments to note the exact position of everything they uncover. Excavations in Inca towns have unearthed pottery and jars, fragments of cloth, jewellery, knives and human burials. They are constantly adding to what we know about the Inca civilization.

STEEP STREETS
Machu Picchu was built on a steep slope, using *mit'a* work. Some of its buildings were set into the rock, while many more were built on raised terraces of stone. Its streets had steps in many places. Incas may have fled to this mountain retreat from Cuzco after the Spanish invaded in 1532. It was abandoned within 40 years and soon covered by creepers and trees.

RUINS OF CHAN CHAN

Chan Chan, capital of Chimor, was built in the north, at the mouth of the Moche River. It was the biggest city of ancient Peru. Far from the granite of the Andes, Chan Chan was constructed with adobe (bricks made from sun-baked mud). The city was laid out in a grid pattern, with 12m/36ft-high compound walls marking out the homes of royalty, nobles and craft workers.

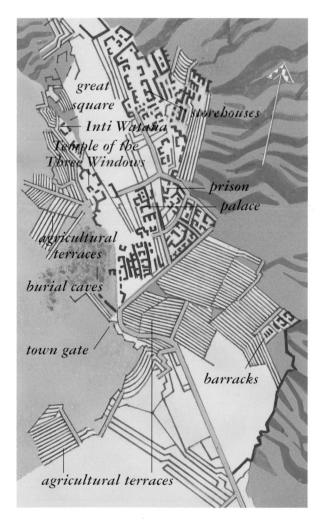

LIVING IN THE CLOUDS

The small but spectacular Inca town of Machu Picchu clings to a high mountain ridge beneath the peak of Wayna Picchu. In about 1450, it had its own ceremonial square, temples and burial caves. The town also had army barracks, public stores, a prison, housing for craft workers and farmers, and a palace for visiting royalty. The town was defended from attack by a twin wall and a ditch.

A PLAN OF THE TOWN

The long and narrow layout of Machu Picchu was decided by its ridge-top location at 2,743m/9,000ft above sea level. The great square was the religious and political heart of the town.

An Inca House

A TYPICAL HOUSE in an Inca town such as Machu Picchu was built from blocks of stone. White granite was the best, being very hard and strong. The roof of each house was pitched at quite a steep angle, so that heavy mountain rains could drain off quickly. Timber roof beams were lashed to stone pegs on the gables, and supported a wooden frame. This was thatched with a tough grass called *ichu*.

Most houses had just one floor, but a few had two or three, joined by rope ladders inside the house or by stone blocks set into the outside wall. Most had a single doorway hung with cloth or hide, and some had an open window on the gable end.

Each building was home to a single family and formed part of a compound. As many as half a dozen houses would be grouped around a shared courtyard. All the buildings belonged to families who were members of the same *ayllu*, or clan.

MUD AND THATCH

Various types of houses were to be seen in different parts of the Inca Empire. Many were built in old-fashioned or in regional styles. These round and rectangular houses in Bolivia are made of mud bricks (adobe). The roofs are thatched with *ichu* grass.

upper floor

inside hearth

courtyard

FLOATING HOMES

These houses are built by the Uru people, who fish in Lake Titicaca and hunt in the surrounding marshes. They live on the lake shore and also on floating islands made of matted *totora* reeds. Their houses are made of *totora* and *ichu* grass. Both these materials would have been used in the Titicaca area in Inca times. The reeds are collected from the shallows and piled onto the floor of the lake. New reeds are constantly added.

PICTURES AND POTTERY
Houses with pitched roofs and windows appear as part of the decoration on this pottery from Pacheco, Nazca. To find out about houses in ancient Peru, historians look at surviving towns and ruins, at housing styles still in use today and at old pictures and designs on objects.

SQUARE STONE, ROUND PEG
Squared-off blocks of stone are called ashlars. These white granite ashlars make up a wall in the Inca town of Pisaq. They are topped by a round stone peg. Pegs like these were probably used to support roof beams or other structures, such as ladders from one floor to another.

gable

roofbeam

roof peg

wall niche

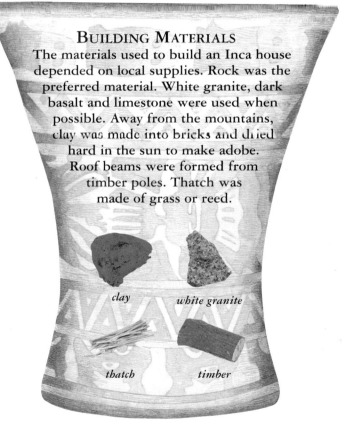

BUILDING MATERIALS
The materials used to build an Inca house depended on local supplies. Rock was the preferred material. White granite, dark basalt and limestone were used when possible. Away from the mountains, clay was made into bricks and dried hard in the sun to make adobe. Roof beams were formed from timber poles. Thatch was made of grass or reed.

clay

white granite

thatch

timber

BUILDING TO LAST
The Incas built simple, but solid, dwellings in the mountains. The massive boulders used for temples and fortresses are here replaced by smaller, neatly cut stones. See how the roof beams are lashed to the gables to support the thatch. Stone roofs were very rare, even on the grandest houses. Timber joists provide an upper floor. The courtyard is used just as much as the inside of the house for everyday living.

Inside the Home

Let's visit the home of an Inca mountain farmer. The outer courtyard is busy, with smoke rising from cooking pots into the fresh mountain air. An elderly woman stacks firewood, while her daughter sorts out bundles of alpaca wool. A young boy brings in a pot of fresh water, splashing the ground as he puts it down.

Pulling aside the cloth at the doorway, you blink in the dark and smoky atmosphere. Cooking has to be done indoors when the weather is poor. The floor of beaten earth is swept clean. There is no furniture at all, but part of the stone wall juts out to form a bench. In one corner there is a clutter of pots and large storage jars. Cloaks and baskets hang from stone pegs on the wall. Niches, inset in the wall, hold a few precious objects and belongings, perhaps a pottery jar or some shell necklaces. Other items include a knife and equipment for weaving or fishing.

Pot Stoves

Cooking stoves of baked clay, very like these, have been used in Peru for hundreds of years. Round cooking pots were placed on top of these little stoves. The fuel was pushed in through a hole in the side. Pot stoves are easily carried and can be used outside. Inside the house, there might be a more permanent hearth, made of clay or stone.

Drink It Up!

The shape of this two-handled jar and its simple tones are typically Inca, but the geometric patterns suggest it may have been the work of a Chimú potter. A jar like this might have been used to carry *chicha* (maize beer) made by the *mamakuna* for one of the great religious festivals. People drank far too much *chicha* on these occasions, and drunkenness was common.

Inside Story

What was it like to live in Machu Picchu 500 years ago? The insides of the remaining buildings give us many clues. Even though the thatched roofs and timbers have been lost over the years, some have been restored. Well over half the buildings in Machu Picchu were homes for ordinary people.

REED MATTING

Totora reed matting, used by the Uru people today, is rolled up in bales by Lake Titicaca. In Inca times, reed mats were used as bedding by most people. They slept fully dressed on the ground. Even the emperor and the nobles slept on the floor, but they had blankets and rugs of the finest cloth to cover themselves. Like the Incas, the Uru people have many household uses for *totora* reed. It is a fuel, its flower is used to make medicines and some parts of it may be eaten.

HOUSEHOLD GOURDS

Decorated gourds are still sold in the highlands of Peru. Gourds are pumpkin-like plants bearing fruits with a hard shell. Gourds were often hollowed out and dried and used by the Incas as simple containers for everyday use around the house. They served as water bottles or pots.

FUEL SUPPLIES

In many parts of the Inca Empire, timber was scarce, and its use was officially limited. Brushwood, sticks and a mountain plant called *llareta* were collected for tinder and fuel. Llama dung was also widely used as a fuel for cooking or for firing pottery. Fires were started with drills. These were sticks rotated at such high speed against another piece of wood that they became very hot indeed and began to smoke.

timber

brushwood

Hunting and Fishing

THE INCAS hunted wild animals for sport as well as for food. Every four years, there was a great public hunt, at which beaters would form a line many kilometres/miles long and comb the countryside for game. The hunters closed in on the animals with dogs. Dangerous animals were hunted, such as bears and pumas (South American cougars or mountain lions), as well as important sources of food such as deer, guanaco (a wild relative of the llama) and partridges. After the hunt, the meat was cut into strips and dried in the sun. Hunting was a pastime of royalty and nobles, but ordinary people could hunt with permission. Every child learned how to use a sling – ideal for killing small birds. Nets were used to catch wildfowl on lakes and marshes. Spears, clubs, bows and arrows were also used.

BEAK AND TACKLE
The Moche fisherman shown on this jar is using a pelican to catch fish for him with its great pouch of a beak. Fishing crews of the coast used cotton lines, fish hooks of copper or bone, harpoons, or cotton nets with gourd floats.

BEYOND THE SURF
A fishing boat made of bound *totora* reed is steered toward the surf at Huancacho, to the north of Trujillo on Peru's north coast. This sight would have been much the same in the days of the Inca Empire. The first view Spanish explorers had of the Inca Empire was of fishing boats and rafts at sea.

SPEARS OF THE NAZCA
A painting on a pottery vase shows two hunters attacking vicuña with spears. It dates from the Nazca civilization, which lasted from about 200BC to AD750. The first Peruvians lived by hunting, but the Inca State depended mainly on farming and fishing for its food. Hunting had become a pastime.

A REED BOAT

You will need: dry straw or hay, scissors, ruler, strong thread or twine, pencil, darning needle, plastic lid, white glue, paintbrush.

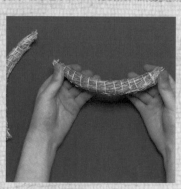

1 Take a fistful of straw or hay and gather it together. Trim one end to make a bundle 20cm/8in long. Make another 20cm/8in bundle and two more 18cm/7in long.

2 Tie a length of thread or twine around one end of a bundle. Then wind it along at 3cm/1¼in intervals. Bind into a point at one end and tie a knot.

3 Gently bend the bound bundle into a banana shape. Tie and bend the remaining three bundles in exactly the same way. Keep the thread tight.

A DAY'S FISHING

Two Moche fishermen sit on a sea-going raft, drinking beer and arguing, no doubt, about the 'fish that got away'. Fishing was already a major occupation on the Peruvian coast about 4,500 years ago. Later coastal peoples, such as the Chimú, specialized as fishermen, supplying the inland cities with their catches. In Inca times, freshly caught fish from the coast were hurried by special messenger to the royal palace at Cuzco.

FISHING IN LAKE AND OCEAN

The cool currents that sweep up the west coast of Peru provide some of the best fishing in all the Pacific Ocean. Small fish such as sardines and anchovies swarm through these waters. Larger fish and shellfish may also be taken. Inland lakes such as Lake Titicaca are also a rich source of fish.

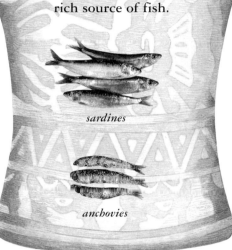

sardines

anchovies

THE CHASE

A picture painted on a *kero* (wooden beaker), shows an Inca hunter bringing down a guanaco. His weapon is the *bola*, a heavy cord weighted with three balls. It was hurled at the guanaco's legs in order to entangle it. The *bola* was also used in Argentina in the 1800s by the cowboys called *gauchos*.

The curving sides and pointed prow of a reed boat were designed to cut through the waves.

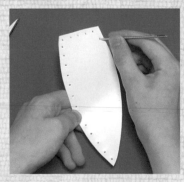

4 Draw a boat shape on plastic, 14cm/5½in long, 6cm/2½in at the widest point and 4cm/1½in at the stern. Cut it out. Prick holes 1cm/½in apart around the edge.

5 Thread the needle and carefully sew one of the shorter bundles to one side of the boat. Repeat on the other side of the boat with the matching bundle.

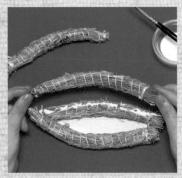

6 Use white glue to attach the longer straw or hay bundles on top of the first ones. Curve the uncut ends upward slightly to form the prow of the boat.

7 Paint the hull of the boat with glue to make it waterproof. Let it dry completely before testing your sea-going craft in a bowl of water!

Living on the Land

THE MOUNTAINS, windy plateaus and deserts of Peru are very difficult to farm. Over thousands of years, humans struggled to tame these harsh landscapes. They brought water to dry areas, dug terraced fields out of steep slopes and improved wild plants such as the potato until they became useful food crops. In Inca times, two-thirds of the farmers' produce was set aside for the emperor and the priests, so there was little personal reward for the people who did the hard work.

Royal officials decided the borders of all the fields and of the pastures for llama and alpaca herds. The soil was broken with hoes and plow-like spades called *takllas*. These simple tools were made of hardened wood. Some were tipped with bronze. The Incas knew how to keep the soil well fertilized, using llama dung in the mountains and guano (seabird droppings) on the coast. In dry areas, the Incas built reservoirs called *qochas* to catch the rain. They were experts at irrigation, carefully controlling water-flow through the fields.

FREEZE-DRIED POTATOES
A woman of the Tinqui people lays out potatoes on the ground, just as farmers would have done in the days of the Incas. Over two hundred potato varieties were grown in the Andes. They were preserved by being left to dry in the hot daytime sun and cold overnight frosts. Dried, pressed potato, called *chuño*, just needed to be soaked to be ready for cooking.

A HIGHLAND CROP
Kinua ripens in the sun. This tough crop can be grown at over 3,800m/12,400ft above sea-level, and can survive both warm days and cold nights. *Kinua* was ideal for the Andes. Its seeds were boiled to make a kind of porridge, and its leaves could be stewed as well.

A SAFE HARVEST
The farmer uses his sling to scare hungry birds from the new corn, while his wife harvests the crop. March was the month when the corn ripened, and April was the month of harvest.

AN ANCIENT PATTERN

Painstaking work over many years created these terraced fields, or *andenes*, near the Inca town of Pisaq. All the soil had to be brought up in baskets from the valley floor far below. Terracing aims to provide a workable depth of level soil, while retaining walls prevent earth from being washed away by the rains. The bottom of each terrace was laid with gravel for good drainage. The Pisaq fields belonged to the emperor and produced corn of the highest quality.

ALL-AMERICAN CROPS

Crops that were once grown in just one part of the world are now grown in other continents as well. Many of the world's most common crops were first grown in the Americas. These include potatoes, tomatoes, corn, cassava, sweet potatoes and squash.

cassava

sweet potatoes

potatoes

squash

MOTHER EARTH

This gold plate, made by the Chimú people, shows the earth goddess surrounded by Peruvian crops, each grouped according to its growing season. They include corn, sweet potato and cassava. The earth goddess was called Pachamama, and she played an especially important part in the religious beliefs of farming villages in the Andes. Most farmers in the Inca Empire spent their lives trying to tame a hostile environment. The fertility of the land was important in religious as well as economic terms.

Food and Feasts

A REGIONAL GOVERNOR might entertain a royal visitor with a banquet of venison (deer meat), roast duck, fresh fish from the lakes or the ocean, and tropical fruits such as bananas and guavas. Honey was used as a sweetener.

Peasants ate squash and other vegetables in a stew, and fish was also eaten where it was available. Families kept guinea pigs for their meat, but most of their food was vegetarian. The bulk of any meal would be made up of starchy foods. These were prepared from grains such as maize or *quinua*, or from root crops such as potatoes, cassava or a highland plant called *oca*. A strong beer called *chicha* was made from maize. The grains were chewed and spat out, then left to ferment in water.

MIXED SPICES
This pottery pestle and mortar may have been used for grinding and mixing herbs. It is about 1,000 years old and was made by the Chimú people. Peruvian dishes were often hot and spicy, using eye-watering quantities of hot chilli peppers. Chilli peppers were one of the first food plants to be cultivated. Peppers of various kinds were grown on the coast and foothills.

MEALS AND MANNERS
Inca nobles ate and drank from wooden plates and painted beakers called *keros*. These continued to be made after the Spanish conquest. Pottery was also used to make beautiful cups and dishes. Most peasants drank and ate from gourds. There were no tables, so food was eaten sitting on the ground. Two main meals were eaten each day, one in the morning and one in the evening.

BEAN STEW
You will need: 250g/9oz/ 1 cup dried haricot (navy) beans, 4 tomatoes, 500g/1¼lb pumpkin, 30ml/2 tbsp paprika, mixed herbs, salt, black pepper, 100g/3¾oz corn, bowl, large and medium pans, knife, chopping board, measuring cup, spoon.

1 Wash the beans in plenty of cold water. Place them in a large bowl and cover them with cold water. Leave them to soak for 3 or 4 hours.

2 Drain the beans and put them in a large pan. Cover them with cold water. Bring to the boil. Simmer for 2 hours or until just tender.

3 While the beans are cooking, chop the tomatoes finely on the chopping board. Peel the pumpkin and cut the flesh into 2cm/¾in cubes.

A TROPICAL MENU

The mountains were cool because they were high. Down on the lowlands it was much hotter, and tropical crops could be grown wherever there was enough water. These included tomatoes, avocados, beans, pumpkin-like squashes, chilli peppers, peanuts and fruits such as guava.

avocado pear

chilli pepper

peanuts

beans

CORN ON THE COB

This maize plant was crafted in Inca silver. The real maize crop would have been almost as precious. Maize could be ground into the flour we call cornmeal, and this was used to make porridge, pancake-like bread and dumplings. The yellow corn could also be toasted, boiled or puffed up into popcorn.

Eat up your stew.... It probably tastes better without the guinea pig meat! Inca food was plain but nourishing.

TO THE LORD OF MAIZE

This maize left in a pottery dish in a Nazca grave is an offering to the Lord of the Maize. Maize played such an important part in the life of Central and South America that it had its own gods, goddesses and festivals.

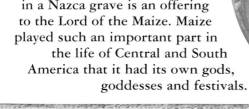

4 Heat 105ml/7 tbsp water in a medium pan. Stir in the paprika and bring to the boil. Add the tomatoes and a sprinkling of herbs, salt and pepper.

5 Simmer for 15 minutes until thick and well blended. Drain the beans and return to the large pan with the pumpkin and the tomato mixture. Stir well.

6 Simmer for 15 minutes. Add the corn and simmer for 5 more minutes until the pumpkin has almost disintegrated and the stew is thick.

7 Taste (but be careful — it's hot!). Add more salt and pepper if necessary. Serve in bowls. Cornbread or tortillas would be an ideal accompaniment.

Textiles and Tunics

IN ALL THE CIVILIZATIONS of the Andes, spinning and weaving were the main household tasks of women of all ranks. Girls learned to weave at an early age, and men wove too. There was a long tradition of embroidery, using bone needles. In Inca times, weaving reached an incredibly high standard. Weaving textiles formed part of the work tax, like farming or building. Woven cloth was stored in government warehouses and used to pay troops and officials.

Inca men wore a loincloth around the waist, secured by a belt. Over this was a simple knee-length tunic, often made of alpaca wool. On cold nights, they might wear a cloak as well. Women wrapped themselves in a large rectangular cloth of alpaca wool, with a sash around the waist and a shawl. There were many kinds of regional headdresses, caps of looped wool, headbands, hats and feathers. Sandals were made of leather or woven grasses.

PINNED IN STYLE
A long decorative pin called a *tupu* was used by the Incas to fasten dresses and shawls. It might be made from copper, silver or gold. This *tupu* was found at the Sacsahuaman fortress in Cuzco.

INCA FASHION
About 500 years ago, this fine tunic belonged to an Inca nobleman from the south coast of Peru. Its design is simple, but it is beautifully decorated with flower and animal designs. Dress was a status symbol in the Inca Empire. The shape of clothes was much the same for all social classes, but the more important you were, the finer the cloth and the decoration.

AN INCA TUNIC
You will need: blue felt 65 x 160cm/26 x 64in, red felt 40cm/16in square, white glue, brush, tape measure, scissors, ruler, pencil, thread or wool, needle, cream calico fabric, acrylic or fabric paints, paintbrush, water pot.

1 Place the blue felt flat on the table. Position the red felt in the middle of it to form a diamond shape. Glue the red felt carefully in place.

2 For the neck opening, cut a slit 22cm/8¾in long through the middle of both layers of material, with the long side of the blue felt towards you.

3 Fold the tunic in half along the slit. Halfway along the slit, cut a 12cm/4¾in slit at right angles to the first. Only cut through one double layer of fabric.

MATERIALS AND DYES

Highland animals provided warm wool. Llamas had the coarsest wool, and vicuñas the softest. Alpaca wool was the one most commonly used. Cotton was grown in the hot lowland regions and was widely worn for its coolness. Plants were used to dye either the yarn or the finished textiles. A scarlet dye called cochineal was obtained from the dried bodies of insects.

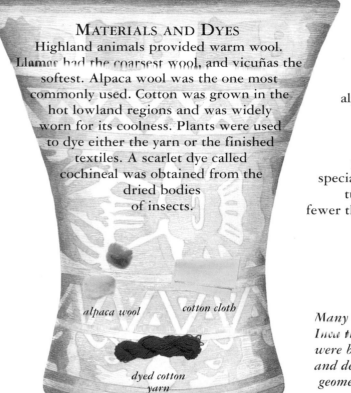

alpaca wool   *cotton cloth*

dyed cotton yarn

SHIMMERING GOLD

For a religious festival, Inca nobles and priests might wear spectacular costumes. This is part of a tunic made of woven alpaca wool decorated with fine gold work. It comes from Peru's south coast. Clothes like these were produced by craftsmen in special workshops. One Chimú tunic was studded with no fewer than 13,000 pieces of gold!

Many Inca tunics were brightly coloured and decorated with geometric patterns.

BACKSTRAPPERS

This Moche painting shows people weaving with backstrap looms. The upright or warp threads are tensioned between an upright post and a beam attached to the weaver's waist. The cross or weft threads are passed in between. Backstrap looms are still used in Central and South America today.

4 Using the thread or wool, sew together the sides of the tunic with large stitches. Leave enough space for armholes at the top.

5 Draw plenty of 5cm/2in squares in pencil on the cream fabric. Paint them in bright, geometric Inca designs. Look at the patterns here for ideas.

6 Allow the paint to dry completely. Then carefully cut out the squares and arrange them in any pattern you like on the front of your tunic.

7 When you have a pattern you are happy with, glue the squares in position. Wait until the glue is dry before trying on your unique Inca tunic.

Jewels and Feathers

FESTIVAL COSTUMES in the Andes today come in dazzling pinks, reds and blues. In the Inca period it was no different. People loved to wear bright braids, threads and ribbons. Sequins, beads, feathers and gold were sewn into fabric, while precious stones, red shells, silver and gold were made into beautiful earplugs, necklaces, pendants, nostril-rings and discs. However, it was only the nobles who were allowed to show off by wearing feathers, jewels and precious metals. Some of the most prized ornaments were gifts from the emperor for high-ranking service in the army.

Much of the finest craft work went into making small statues and objects for religious ceremonies, temples and shrines. During the Inca period, craft workers were employed by the State. They produced many beautiful treasures, but some of the best of these were the work of non-Inca peoples, particularly the Chimú. Treasures shipped to Spain after the Conquest astounded the Europeans by their fine craftsmanship.

PLUMES OF THE CHIEF
An impressive headdress like this would have belonged to a high-ranking Inca official or general in northern Chile over 500 years ago. The hat is made from coils of dyed llama wool. It is decorated with bold designs, and topped by a spray of feathers.

A SACRED PUMA
This gold pouch in the shape of a puma, a sacred animal, was made by the Moche people between 1,300 and 1,700 years ago. It may have been used to carry *coca* leaves. These were used as a drug during religious ceremonies. The pattern on the body is made up of two-headed snakes.

A GOLD AND SILVER NECKLACE
You will need: self-drying clay, cutting board, ruler, large blunt needle, gold and silver paint, paintbrush, water pot, thin card, pencil, scissors, strong thread.

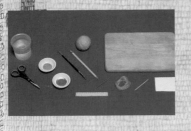

1 Form pieces of clay into beads in the shape of monkey nuts. You will need 10 beads about 3.5 x 2cm/1½ x ¾in, and 10 beads about 2.5 x 1.5cm/1 x ½in.

2 Use the needle to mark patterns on the beads, so that they look like nut shells. Then carefully make a hole through the middle of each bead. Leave to dry.

3 Paint half the shells of each size gold and half of them silver. You should have 5 small and 5 large gold beads, and 5 small and 5 large silver beads.

PRECIOUS AND PRETTY

The most valued stone in the Andes was blue-green turquoise. It was cut and polished into beads and discs for necklaces, and inlaid in gold statues and masks. Blue lapis lazuli, black jet and other stones also found their way along trading routes. Colombia, on the northern edge of the Inca Empire, mined many precious stones and metals. Seashells were cut and polished into beautiful beads.

emerald   *turquoise*

lapis lazuli

BIRDS OF A FEATHER

Birds and fish decorate this feather cape. It was made by the Chancay people of the central Peruvian coast between the 1300s and 1500s. It would have been worn for religious ceremonies. Feather work was a skilled craft in both Central and South America. In Inca times, the vivid feathers of birds called macaws were sent to the emperor as tribute from the tribes of the Amazon forests.

Necklaces made of gold, silver and jewels would only have been worn by Inca royalty, perhaps the Quya herself.

TREASURE LOST AND FOUND

A beautifully made gold pendant created in the Moche period before the Incas rose to power. After the Spanish conquest of Peru, countless treasures were looted from temples or palaces by Spanish soldiers. Gold was melted down or shipped back to Europe. A few items escaped by being buried in graves. Some have been discovered by archaeologists.

4 Paint some card gold on both sides. On it draw 11 rectangles (3 x 1cm/1¼ x ½in) with rounded ends. Cut them out and carefully prick a hole in each end.

5 Thread the needle and make a knot 10cm/4in from the end of the thread. Then thread the card strips and large beads alternately, using the gold beads first.

6 Be sure to start and end with card strips. When you have finished, knot the thread next to the last card strip. Cut the thread 10cm/4in from the knot.

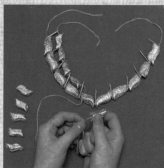

7 Repeat steps 5 and 6 using more thread and the small beads, so that the beads are joined as shown. Finally, knot the ends of the two threads together.

35

Everyday Crafts

MANY BEAUTIFUL OBJECTS produced in the Inca Empire were not made of gold and jewels but of simpler, more down-to-earth materials. Baskets and reed mats were made in early prehistoric times by plaiting and twining various materials. All kinds of small objects, such as bowls, pins, spoons and figures, were carved from bone, stone and wood.

Pottery was being made in Peru by about 2000BC, rather later than in the lands to the north and east. It had a great impact on the way people lived because it affected the production, storage, transportation and cooking of food.

South American potters did not shape their pots on a wheel. They built them up in layers from coils of clay. The coils were smoothed out by hand or with tools, marked or painted, dried in the sun and then baked hard.

Many of the pre-Incan civilizations of the Andes produced beautiful pottery. The Nazca often used bold geometric patterns, while the Moche loved to make jars in the shape of animals and people. Many pots were specially made for religious ceremonies.

POLISHED WOOD
This fine black *kero* (drinking vessel) was made by an Inca craftsman. It is of carved and polished wood. Timber was always scarce in the Inca Empire, but wood was widely used to make plates and cups. Rearing up over the rim of the beaker is a fierce-looking big cat, perhaps a puma or a jaguar.

SHAPED FROM CLAY
A fierce puma bares his teeth. He was made from pottery between AD500 and 800. The hole in his back was used to waft clouds of incense during religious ceremonies in the city of Tiwanaku, near Lake Titicaca.

A TIWANAKU POTTERY JAGUAR

You will need: chicken wire, wire-cutters, ruler, newspaper, scissors, white glue, masking tape, flour, water, thin card, paint, water pot, paintbrush.

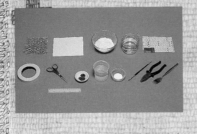

1 Cut a rectangle of chicken wire 14cm/5½in long and 20cm/8in wide. Carefully wrap it around to form a sausage shape. Close one end neatly.

2 Squeeze the other end of the sausage to form the jaguar's neck and head. Fold over the wire at the end to make a neat, round shape for his nose.

3 Make rolls of newspaper about 2.5cm/1in long to form the jaguar's legs. Use strips of paper and glue to join them securely to the jaguar's body as shown.

PRETTY POLLY

This pottery jar, like many from Peru, comes with a handle and a spout. It is shaped and painted to look like a parrot and was made, perhaps 1,000 years before the Incas, by the Nazca potters of southern Peru.

IN THE POTTER'S WORKSHOP

The potter needed a good supply of sticky clay and plenty of water. He also needed large supplies of firewood or dung for fuel. The potter would knead the clay until it was soft and workable. Sometimes he would mix in sand or crushed shells from the coast to help strengthen the clay. Pigments for painting the pottery were made from plants and minerals.

shells *sand*

clay

WATER OF LIFE

This Inca bottle is carved with a figure inside a tower collecting water. No community could survive very long without a good supply of fresh water. Many pots, bottles and beakers from the South American civilizations are decorated with light-hearted scenes of everyday activities. They give us a vivid idea of how people used to live.

The handle and spout design of your Tiwanaku jaguar is known as a stirrup pot, because the arrangement looks rather like the stirrup of a horse.

4 Mix the flour and water to a paste. Use it to glue a layer of newspaper strips all over the jaguar's body. Allow this to dry. You will need three layers.

5 Cut ears from card. Fix on with masking tape. Tape on rolls of newspaper to make the handle, spout and tail as in the finished pot above.

6 Leave the model in a warm and airy place to dry. Then paint it all over with reddish brown paint. Allow the paint to dry completely.

7 Use black paint and a fine brush to decorate the jaguar as shown in the picture. When the paint is dry, varnish with white glue if you wish.

Metals and Mining

THE WHOLE REGION of the Andes had a very long history of metalworking. A stone bowl that was discovered in the Andahuaylas Valley was nearly 3,500 years old. It contained metalworking equipment and finely beaten gold foil. Braziers found at the town of Machu Picchu, from the end of the Inca period, included traces of molten metal.

The Incas often referred to gold as 'sweat of the Sun' and to silver as 'tears of the Moon'. These metals were sacred not only to the gods but also to their descendants on Earth, the *Sapa Inca* and the *Quya*. At the Temple of the Sun in Cuzco, there was a whole garden made of gold and silver, with golden soil, golden stalks of maize and golden llamas. Imagine how it must have gleamed in the sunshine. Copper, however, was used by ordinary people. It was made into cheap adornments, weapons and everyday tools. The Incas' love of gold and silver eventually led to their downfall, for it was reports of their fabulous wealth that lured the Spanish to invade the region.

A SICAN LORD

A ceremonial knife with a crescent-shaped blade is called a *tumi*. Its gold handle is made in the shape of a nobleman or ruler. He wears an elaborate headdress and large discs in his ears. It was made between 1100 and 1300. The knife is in the style of the Sican civilization, which grew up after the decline of the Moche civilization in the AD700s.

A CHIMÚ DOVE

Chimú goldsmiths, the best in the Empire, made this plump dove. When the Incas conquered Chimor in 1470, they forced many thousands of skilled craftsmen from the city of Chan Chan to resettle in the Cuzco area and continue their work.

A TUMI KNIFE

You will need: cardboard, ruler, pencil, scissors, self-drying clay, cutting board, rolling pin, shaping and cutting tools, white glue, gold paint, paintbrush, water pot, blue metallic paper.

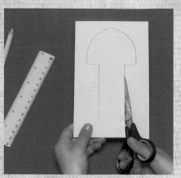

1 On cardboard, draw a knife and cut it out. The rectangular part should be 9 x 3.5cm/3½ x 1½in. The rounded part is 7cm/2¾in across and 4.5cm/1¾in high.

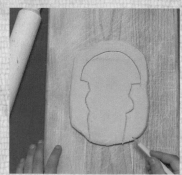

2 Roll out a slab of clay 1cm/½in thick. Draw a *tumi* shape on it. It should be 12.5cm/5in long and measure 9cm/3½in across the widest part at the top.

3 Use the cutting tool to cut around the shape you have drawn. Carefully take away the leftover clay. Make sure the edges are clean and smooth.

MINERAL WEALTH

To this day, the Andes are very rich in minerals. The Incas worked with gold, silver, platinum and copper. They knew how to make alloys, which are mixtures of different metals. Bronze was made by mixing copper and tin. However, unlike their Spanish conquerors, the Incas knew nothing of iron and steel. This put them at a disadvantage when fighting the Europeans.

copper

silver

gold

PANNING FOR GOLD

A boy worker in modern Colombia pans for gold. Some Inca gold was mined, but large amounts also came from panning mountain rivers and streams in the Andes. The river bed was loosened with sticks, and then the water was sifted through shallow trays in search of any flecks of the precious metal that had been washed downstream.

INCA FIGURES

Small ritual figures of women and men from about 6cm/2½in high were often made in the Inca period. They were hammered from sheets of silver and gold and were dressed in miniature versions of adult clothing. They have been found on mountain-top shrine sites in the south-central Andes, in carved stone boxes in Lake Titicaca and at important temples.

The Chimú gold and turquoise tumi *was used by priests at religious ceremonies. It may have been used to kill sacrifices.*

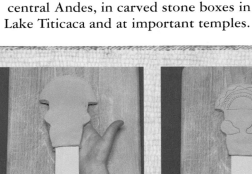

4 Cut a slot into the bottom edge of the clay shape. Lifting it carefully, slide the knife blade into the slot. Use glue to make the joint secure.

5 Use a shaping tool to mark the details of the god on to the clay. Look at the finished knife above to see how to do this. Leave everything to dry.

6 When the clay has hardened, paint the whole knife with gold paint. Leave it to dry completely before painting the other side as well.

7 The original knife was decorated with turquoise. Glue small pieces of blue metallic paper on to the handle as shown in the picture above.

Gods and Spirits

THE FIRST PERUVIANS worshipped nature spirits and creatures such as condors, snakes and jaguars. Later peoples began to believe in gods. Some said the world had been created by the god Wiraqocha, the 'old man of the sky'. He had made the Sun, Moon and stars, and the other gods. He had carved stone statues and made them live, creating the first humans. Myths tell that he sailed away across the Pacific Ocean.

To the Inca people, the most important god was Inti, the Sun. He was the bringer of warmth and light and the protector of the Inca people. Inti's sister and wife was Mamakilya, the silver Moon goddess.

Other gods included Pachamama the Earth goddess, Mamacocha goddess of the sea, Kuychi the Rainbow god and Apu Illapu, god of thunder.

THE GATEWAY GOD
Tiwanaku's 1,400-year-old Gateway of the Sun, in Bolivia, is carved from solid rock and is over 3m/10ft high. The figure may represent the Chavín Staff god or Wiraqocha. It may be a Sun god, for his headdress is made up of rays.

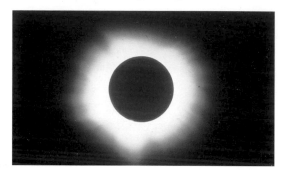

END OF THE WORLD?
The Incas believed that Inti, the Sun god, dropped into the ocean each evening, swam underneath the Earth and appeared next morning in the east, above the mountains. An eclipse of the Sun was a terrifying experience, a warning that Inti was abandoning the emperor and his people.

SPIRITS OF THE MAIZE
On this pottery jar, three gods are shown bursting out of bundles of corn cobs. The jar was made by Moche potters between AD300 and AD700. To all the South American peoples, the world of nature was filled with spiritual forces. They believed that the success of the harvest depended on the good will of the gods.

A GOLD SUN GOD MASK

You will need: large piece of cardboard, pencil, ruler, scissors, white glue, paintbrush, water pot, gold and black paint.

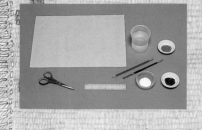

1 Draw a mask on card as shown, 60cm/24in wide and 60cm/24in high. The side pieces are 40cm/16in high. The narrowest part is 8cm/3in wide.

2 Draw zigzag patterns all around the edge of the mask as shown in the picture above. These patterns represent the powerful rays of the Sun.

3 Carefully cut out the whole mask shape. Then cut out the rays around the edge, making sure you don't snip all the way through by mistake.

ANCIENT SECRETS

A mysterious figure, carved from a great stone pillar, stands amid the ruined temples of Tiwanaku. It holds a banded *kero* or drinking cup in its left hand and a sceptre in its right. Is this the figure of an ancient god? The monument is 7.3m/ 24ft tall and was excavated in 1932. It dates back over 1,500 years, to the days when Tiwanaku became a great religious hub.

A GOLDEN MASK

Gold face-masks were made by several Peruvian peoples, including the Nazca and the Inca. Some were used during festivals in praise of the Sun. Others were laid on the faces of the dead, just as they were in ancient Egypt. This fine mask was made by Moche goldsmiths in about AD400.

Hail to Inti, the Sun god! Your mask looks as if it is made from shining gold, the magical metal of the Sun.

WORSHIPPING THE SUN

A golden face in a sunburst represents Inti, god of the Sun. This picture from the 1700s imagines how the *Coricancha*, the Temple of the Sun, in Cuzco, must have appeared 200 years earlier. It shows the *Sapa Inca* making an offering of maize beer to Inti in the great hall.

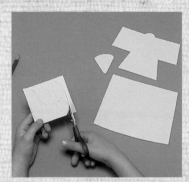

4 Cut out a rectangle of card 15 x 13cm/6 x 5in. Cut a T-shaped piece 14cm/ 5½in across and 11cm/4½in high. Cut out the shapes of eyes, a nose and a mouth.

5 Glue the shapes on to the middle of the mask to form the Sun god's face as shown. Leave the mask flat until the glue is completely dry.

6 Make sure your table top is protected. Cover the whole of the surface of the mask with gold paint. The rays around the edge are fiddly to paint.

7 Finally, use black paint and a fine brush to draw around the face. Add ears and teeth. Decorate the top part with black paint, too.

Temples and Sacrifices

THE INCAS had many *waq'as* (holy places). Some of these shrines were simply streams, rocks or caves that had been visited by pilgrims for thousands of years. Others were wayside idols, or temples built long before the Incas came to power. In Chavín de Huantar, temples were built between 900 and 200BC. They were decorated with carvings of fantastic jaguars and birds of prey. Massive pyramid temples and platforms had been built on the coastal plains. Huaca del Sol, at the Moche capital of Cerro Blanco, was made from over 100 million mud bricks. The Incas themselves built many temples dedicated to the gods Inti, Mama Killa, Wiraqocha and Apu Illapa.

The *Willak Umu* (Inca High Priest) was a member of the royal family. Priests made offerings to the gods and took drugs that gave them dreams and visions. They looked for omens – signs to help them see the future.

HUACA EL DRAGON
Fantastic figures in dried mud decorate Huaca el Dragon, a pyramid burial site to the north-west of Chan Chan. It was a religious site of the Chimú people about 800 years ago, before the Inca Empire.

OFFERINGS TO THE GODS
Llamas are chosen to be sacrificed to the gods. White llamas were offered to the Sun god, Inti, brown ones to the creator god, Wiraqocha, and spotted ones to Apu Illapa, a thunder god. Their entrails were examined for omens. Guinea pigs were also sacrificed. Other offerings to the gods included food, *chicha* beer, maize and cloth. Many offerings were burnt on a fire.

GATEWAY OF THE SUN
The city of Tiwanaku, with its great ceremonial arch, was the site of many religious activities. It had a raised platform, 15m/50ft high, and archaeologists have found the remains of offerings and human sacrifices there. Tiwanaku beliefs seem to have been similar to those of the Wari city-state.

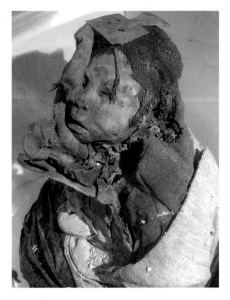

AT PACHACAMAC

Pachacamac, near Lima, was a site of pilgrimage in Inca times. It was named after Pachacamac, a much older creator god. Under Topa Inka, the Incas adopted Pachacamac as their own, worshipping him as a god of fire. They came to Pachacamac to have their fortunes told by an oracle. The site had a pyramid and many shrines. This is the Temple of the Virgins.

HUMAN SACRIFICE

When a new emperor came to the throne, or during times of crisis, Inca priests sacrificed hundreds of people. Victims had to be pure and perfect to please the gods. Boys or girls, *akllakuna*, or sometimes adults were chosen. This girl was one of three sacrificed on a peak in northern Argentina. Her remains were discovered in 1999.

TEMPLES OF THE SUN

The *Coricancha*, or Temple of the Sun, in Cuzco, was the holiest shrine in the Inca Empire. Its remains are seen here topped by a Christian church that was built by the Spanish in 1650. Inca priests believed that power lines called *ceques* radiated out from the *Coricancha*, linking holy sites across the Empire. There were other great Sun temples, too. One was on an island in Lake Titicaca, another was at Vilcashuaman, and a third was near Aconcagua, the highest peak in all the Americas.

Medicine and Magic

LIKE MOST PEOPLES in the world five hundred years ago, the Incas and the other locals had some idea of science or medicine. However, curing people was believed to be chiefly a matter of religious rituals and magical spells. No doubt some of these did help people to feel better. Curing sick people was the job either of priests, or of the local healer or medicine man.

As in Europe at that time, Inca healers used fasting and blood-letting (allowing blood to flow from a cut) for many cures. They also tried blood transfusion (putting new blood into someone's body). They succeeded in this far earlier than doctors in other parts of the world, because peoples of the Andes shared the same blood group. The Incas could also set broken bones, amputate limbs, treat wounds and pull teeth. Medicines were made from herbs, roots, leaves and powders.

THE MEDICINE MAN
This Moche healer or priest, from about AD500, seems to be going into a trance and listening to the voices of spirits or gods. He may be trying to cure a sick patient, or he may be praying over the patient's dead body.

MAGIC DOLLS
Model figures like this one, made from cotton and reed, are often found in ancient graves in the Chancay River region. They are often called dolls, but it seems unlikely that they were ever used as toys. They were probably believed to have magical qualities. The Chancay people may have believed that the dolls helped the dead person in another world.

CARRYING COCA
Small bags like these were used for carrying medicines and herbs, especially coca. The leaves of the coca plant were widely used to stimulate the body and to kill pain. Coca is still widely grown in the Andes today. It is used to make the illegal drug cocaine.

MEDICINE BAG
You will need: scissors, cream calico fabric, pencil, ruler, paintbrush, water pot, acrylic or fabric paints, black, yellow, green and red wool, white glue, needle and thread, masking tape.

1 Cut two 20cm/8in squares of fabric. Draw a pattern of stripes and diamonds on the fabric and use acrylic or fabric paints to paint them.

2 For the tassels, cut about 10 pieces of wool 8cm/3¼in long. Fold a piece of wool 15cm/6in long in half. Loop it around each tassel as shown above.

3 Wind a matching piece of wool, 50cm/20in long, around the end of the tassel. When you have finished, knot the wool and tuck the ends inside.

HERBAL REMEDIES

Drugs widely used in ancient Peru included the leaves of tobacco and coca plants. A yellow-flowered plant called calceolaria was used to cure infections. Cinchona bark produced quinine, a medicine we use today to treat malaria. That illness only arrived in South America after the Spanish conquest. However, quinine was used earlier to treat fevers. Suppliers of herbal medicines were known as *hampi kamayuq*.

cinchona tree   tobacco plant

SKULL SURGERY

Nazca surgeons were able to carry out an operation called trepanation. This involved drilling a hole in the patient's skull in an attempt to relieve pressure on the brain. The Incas believed this released evil spirits. A small silver plate was sometimes fitted over the hole as a protection.

Doctor on call! An Inca medicine chest took the form of a woven bag, carried on the shoulder.

A BAD OMEN

A comet shoots across the night sky. The Incas believed such sights would bring plague or disease in their wake. Other common causes of illness were believed to include witchcraft, evil spirits and a failure to please the gods. People tried to make themselves better by making offerings to the gods at *waq'as* (local shrines). Healers used charms or spells to keep their patients free from evil spirits.

4 Make nine tassels in all. Place them in groups of three along the bottom of the unpainted side of one of the pieces of fabric. Use glue to fix them in place.

5 Allow the glue to dry. Place the unpainted sides of the fabric pieces together. Sew around the edges as shown. Leave the top edge open.

6 Make a strap by braiding together strands of wool as shown. Cross each outer strand in turn over the middle strand. Tape will help keep the work steady.

7 Knot the ends of the strap firmly. Attach them to both sides of the top of the bag with glue. Make sure the glue is dry before you pick the bag up.

Inca Knowledge

INCA MATHEMATICIANS used the decimal system, counting in tens. To help with their arithmetic, people placed pebbles or grains of maize in counting frames. These had up to twenty sections. *Quipu* strings were also used to record numbers. Strings were knotted to represent units, tens, hundreds, thousands or even tens of thousands.

The Incas worked out calendars of twelve months by observing the Sun, Moon and stars as they moved across the sky. They knew that these movements marked regular changes in the seasons. They used the calendar to tell them when to plant crops. Inca priests set up stone pillars outside the city of Cuzco to measure the movements of the Sun.

As in Europe at that time, astronomy, which is the study of the stars, was confused with astrology, which is the belief that the stars and planets influence human lives. Incas saw the night sky as being lit up by gods and mythical characters.

FORTUNES FROM THE STARS AND PLANETS
An Inca astrologer observes the position of the Sun. The Incas believed that careful watching of the stars and planets revealed their influence on our lives. For example, the star pattern or constellation that we call the Lyre was known to the Incas as the Llama. It was believed that it influenced llamas and those who herded them.

THE SUN STONE
A stone pillar called *Inti Watana* (Tethering Post of the Sun) stood at the eastern edge of the great square in Machu Picchu. It was like a giant sundial and the shadows it cast confirmed the movements of the Sun across the sky – a matter of great practical and religious importance.

A QUIPU
You will need: scissors, rope and string of various thicknesses, a 90cm/36in length of thick rope, paints, paintbrush, water pot.

1 Cut the rope and string into about 15 lengths measuring from 20cm/8in to 80cm/32in. Paint them in various bright shades. Leave them to dry completely.

2 To make the top part of the *quipu*, take a piece of thick rope, about 90cm/36in long. Tie a knot in each end as shown in the picture above.

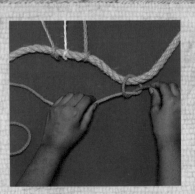

3 Next, take pieces of thinner rope or string of various lengths and shades. Tie them along the thicker rope, so that they all hang on the same side.

THE MILKY WAY

On dark nights, Inca priests looked for the band of stars that we call the Milky Way. They called it *Mayu* (Heavenly River) and used it to make calculations about seasons and weather conditions. In its darker spaces they saw the shadow of the Rain god Apu Illapu. The shape of the Milky Way was believed to mirror that of the Inca Empire.

SUN WATCH

The *Inti Watana* (Tethering Post of the Sun) at Machu Picchu was one of many Sun stones across the Empire. *Sukana* (stone pillars) near Cuzco showed midsummer and midwinter sun positions. The Sun god, Inti, was believed to live in the north and go south each summer.

KEEPERS OF THE QUIPU

Vast amounts of information could be stored on a *quipu*. A large one might have up to 2,000 cords. The *quipu* was rather like an Inca version of the computer, only the memory had to be provided by the operator's brain rather than a silicon chip. Learning the *quipu* code of colours, knots, and major and minor strings took many years. Expert operators were called *quipu-kamayuq*.

You have now designed a simple quipu. Can you imagine designing a system that would record the entire population of a town, their ages, the taxes they have paid and the taxes they owe? The Incas did just that!

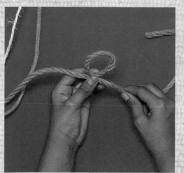

4 Tie knots in the thinner ropes or strings. One knot you might like to try begins by making a loop of rope as shown in the picture above.

5 Pass one end of the rope through the loop. Pull the rope taut but don't let go of the loop. Repeat this step until you have a long knot. Pull it tight.

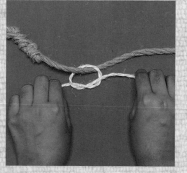

6 Make different sizes of knots on all the ropes or strings. Each knot could represent a family member, school lesson or other important detail.

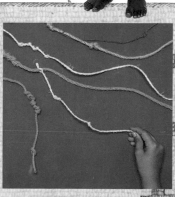

7 Add some more strings to the knotted strings. Your *quipu* may be seen by lots of people. Only you will know what the ropes, strings and knots mean!

51

Married Life

WEDDINGS WERE SOME of the happiest occasions in an Inca village. They offered a chance for the whole community to take time off work. The day was celebrated with dancing, music and feasting. The groom would probably be 25 years of age, at which point he was regarded as an adult citizen, and his bride would be rather younger – about 20.

For the first year of the marriage, a couple did not have to pay any tax either in goods or work. However, most of their lives would be spent working hard. When they were elderly, they would still be expected to help with household chores. Later still, when they became too old or sick to look after themselves, they received free food and clothes from the State warehouse. They would then be cared for by their clan or family group.

Not everyone was expected to get married. The *mamakuna* (virgins of the Sun) lived rather like nuns, in a special convent in Cuzco. They wove fine cloth and carried out religious duties. No men were allowed to enter the *mamakuna*'s building.

WEDDING CLOTHES
An Inca nobleman would get married in a very fine tunic. This one is from the southern coast of Peru. Commoners had to wear simpler clothes, but couples were presented with free new clothes from the State warehouses when they married.

MARRIAGE PROSPECTS
Two Inca noble women are painted on the side of this *kero* (wooden beaker). Women of all social classes were only allowed to marry with the approval of their parents and of State officials. They were expected to remain married for life and divorce was forbidden. If either the husband or wife was unfaithful, he or she could face trial and might even be put to death.

REAL PEOPLE
This jar from the Moche period is over 1,300 years old. Unlike the portraits on many jars, it seems to show a real person sitting down and thinking about life. It reminds us that ancient empires were made up of individuals who fell in love, raised children and grew old, just as people do today.

A ROYAL MARRIAGE

A prince of the emperor's family marries in Cuzco. The scene is imagined by an artist of the 1800s. An emperor had many secondary wives in addition to his sister-empress. Between them they produced very many princes and princesses. Inca royal famiies were divided by jealousy and by complicated relations, which often broke out in open warfare. The emperor ordered his officials to keep tight control over who married whom. His own security on the throne depended on it.

A HOME OF THEIR OWN

When a couple married, they left their parents' houses and moved into their own home, like this one at Machu Picchu. The couple now took official control of the fields they would work. These had been allocated to the husband when he was born. Most couples stayed in the area occupied by their own clan, so their relatives would remain nearby.

HIS AND HERS

The everyday lives of most married couples in the Inca Empire were taken up by hard work. Men and women were expected to do different jobs. Women made the *chicha* beer and did the cooking, weaving and some field work. Men did field work and fulfilled the *mit'a* work tax in service to the Inca State. They might build irrigation channels or repair roads.

An Inca Childhood

ANEWBORN INCA BABY was immediately washed in cold water and wrapped in a blanket. It was breast-fed at three set times each day, but cuddling was frowned upon.

Babyhood ended with a naming ceremony at the age of two, during which a lock of hair was cut off. The toddler still spent a lot of time playing – spinning tops were a popular toy. From now on, however, both boys and girls would be expected to start helping out around the house.

Girls came of age at 14. Royal officials decided whether they would become *akllakuna*. Those selected went for training in Cuzco, while the rest remained in their villages. Boys also came of age at 14 and were given a loincloth as a mark of manhood. Boys from noble families were put through special tests of endurance and knowledge. They were then given the weapons and the earplugs that showed their rank in society.

THREE FOR THE POT
A young Inca has been helping out by herding llamas in the mountains. He has taken a net along and caught some wildfowl in the reeds beside the lake. Contemporary pictures like this show that children and teenagers seem to have led a tough, open-air life.

HARD TIMES
Children were often punished severely. Even noble children could expect to be beaten by their teacher on the soles of their feet if they didn't work hard. There were laws to protect children from violence and kidnapping, but in times of famine or war children must have suffered dreadfully.

ROCK-A-BYE BABY
At the age of four days, a baby was wrapped up in swaddling clothes and tied into its *quiru* (wooden cradle). This could be placed on the ground and rocked, or tied on the mother's back. After a few months, the baby was taken from the cradle and left in a special pit, which served as a playpen.

Learning to Spin Yarn

Inca girls were taught to spin using a drop spindle and a distaff, a stick round which they wound the prepared fleece or cotton. Using the right hand they twisted the spindle with its whirling weight attached. They guided the threads from the distaff with the left hand. The thread was twisted into yarn, which was used for weaving on a backstrap loom. The hunchbacked woman in this drawing is spinning as she walks along the road. She was trained in her youth to be a useful member of Inca society.

Helping in the Fields

This Inca boy has a sling and is attacking the flocks of birds that are robbing the maize fields in his village. Both boys and girls were expected to help with the farming and to learn working skills from their parents, such as weaving or terrace-building. Most children in the Inca Empire did not go to school but were educated by their families. They learned what they needed for adult life and no more. The same was true in most parts of the world 500 years ago.

Going to School

This building at Laris, near Cuzco is a school. Before the Spanish invasion, there was little formal education in Peru. Teenage boys from noble families were taught in Cuzco. Their timetable included Quechua language in Year One, Inca religion and astronomy in Year Two, arithmetic, geometry and *quipu* studies in Year Three, and history in Year Four. *Quipus* were knotted strings used to record information. Pupils also studied music, poetry and the geography of Tawantinsuyu. The only girls to receive formal education were the *akllakuna*, who were taught weaving, cooking and religious studies.

Land of the Dead

ARCHAEOLOGISTS HAVE FOUND many burial sites in the Andes. Bodies are most easily preserved in very dry or very cold conditions, and this region has both. As early as 3200BC, the Andean peoples learned how to embalm or mummify bodies. The insides were often taken out and buried. The rest of the body was dried, and the eyes were replaced with shells. When an Inca emperor died, his mummified body was kept in his former palace. The body was waited on by his descendants and even taken out to enjoy festivals! Respect for ancestors was an important part of Inca religious beliefs.

Inca funerals were sad occasions with slow music. Women cut off their long hair as a sign of grief. When the emperor died, some of his wives and servants were killed. The Incas believed that good people went to *Hanakpacha*, the Empire of the Sun, after death. Bad people had a wretched afterlife, deep in the Earth.

FACING THE NEXT WORLD
Many South American mummies were buried in a sitting position. Their knees were drawn up and bound into position with cord. Over their faces were masks of wood, clay or gold, depending on their status. This mask, perhaps from the pre-Incan Nazca period, was decorated with bright feathers.

THE LORD OF SIPÁN
In 1988, a Peruvian archaeologist called Dr Walter Alva opened up a royal tomb at Sipán, near Chiclayo in northern Peru. The 'Lord of Sipán' had been buried there with his servants, amid treasures made of gold, silver, copper and precious stones. The tomb belonged to the Moche civilization, which flourished between AD1 and 700.

A CHANCAY GRAVE DOLL
You will need: scissors, cream calico fabric, pencil, ruler, paints, paintbrush, water pot, black wool, white glue, padding, 20 red pipecleaners, red wool.

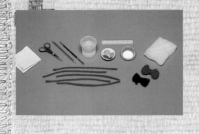

1 Cut two fabric rectangles 16 x 11cm/6½ x 4½in for the body. Cut two shield-shaped pieces 7cm/2¾in wide and 8cm/3¼in long for the head. Paint one side.

2 Cut 35 strands of black wool, each 18cm/7¼in long, for the doll's hair. Glue them evenly along the top of the wrong side of the unpainted face shape.

3 Cut a piece of padding slightly smaller than the face. Glue it on top of the hair and face below. Then glue the painted face on top. Leave to dry.

TOWERS OF THE DEAD

Various South American peoples left mummies in stone towers called *chullpas*, such as these ones at Nina Marca. Goods were placed in the towers for the dead person to use in the next life. These included food and drink, pins, pots, knives, mirrors and clothes. Discoveries of the goods left in graves have helped archaeologists find out about everyday life long ago.

FACE OF THE MUMMY

This head belonged to a body that was mummified over 1,400 years ago in the Nazca desert. The skin is leathery, and the mouth gapes open in a lifelike manner. Most extraordinary is the skull's high, domed forehead. This shows that the dead person had his head bound with cloth as a small child. An elongated head was a sign of status amongst the Nazca people.

DEATH WITH REVERENCE

This face mask of beaten gold dates back to the 1100s or 1200s, during the Inca Empire. Its eyes are made of emerald, and it is decorated with pendants and a nose ornament. The crest on top, decorated with animal designs, serves as a crown or headdress. This mask was made by a Chimú goldsmith and laid in a royal grave.

Dolls like these were probably placed in the graves of the Chimú people. They would serve as helpers in the life to come.

4 For each arm, take five pipecleaners and cut them to 11cm/4½in. Twist them together to within 1.5cm/½in of one end. Splay this end to make fingers.

5 Make legs in the same way, but this time twist all the way and bend the ends to make feet. Wind wool around the arms and legs to hide the twists.

6 Assemble the doll as in the picture. Use glue to fix the arms and legs and padding between the body pieces. Glue the front piece of the body in place.

7 Use glue to fix the head to the front of the body, making sure the hair does not become caught. Leave the doll to dry completely before picking it up.

Warriors and Weapons

THE INCA EMPIRE was brought about and held together by military force. Its borders were defended by a string of forts. The cities served as walled refuges when the surrounding countryside was under attack from enemies. There was a standing army of some 10,000 elite troops, but the great bulk of soldiers were conscripts, paying their State dues by serving out their *mit'a*. Badges and headdresses marked the rank of officers. In the 1500s women joined in the resistance to the Spanish conquest, using slings to devastating effect. The Incas were fierce fighters, but they stood no chance against the guns and steel of the Spanish.

TAKE THAT!
This star may have looked pretty, but it was deadly when whirled from the leather strap. It was made of obsidian, a glassy black volcanic rock. Inca warriors also fought with spikes set in wooden clubs, and some troops favoured the *bolas*, corded weights that were also used in hunting. Slings were used for scaring the birds. However, in the hands of an experienced soldier, they could be used to bring down a hail of stones on enemies and crack their heads open.

WAITING FOR THE CHARGE
A Moche warrior goes down on one knee and brings up his shield to defend himself. He is bracing himself for an enemy charge. All South American armies fought on foot. The horse was not seen in Peru until the Spanish introduced it.

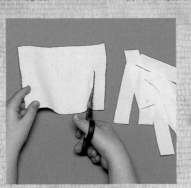

IN THE BARRACKS
Many towns of the Inca Empire were garrisoned by troops. These restored barrack blocks at Machu Picchu may once have housed conscripted soldiers serving out their *mit'a*. They would have been inspected by a high-ranking general from Cuzco. During the Spanish invasion, it is possible that Machu Picchu became a base for desperate resistance fighters.

AN INCA HELMET
You will need: scissors, cream calico fabric, ruler, balloon, white glue, paintbrush, paints, water pot, yellow and black felt, black wool.

1 Cut the fabric into strips about 8 x 2cm/3¼ x ¾in as shown. You will need enough to cover the top half of a blown-up balloon three times.

2 Blow up the balloon to the same size as your head. Glue the strips of fabric over the top half. Leave each layer to dry before adding the next.

3 When the last layer is dry, pop the balloon and carefully pull it away. Use scissors to trim round the edge of the helmet. Paint it a reddish orange.

KINGS OF THE CASTLE

The massive fortress of Sacsahuaman at Cuzco was built on a hill. One edge was formed by a cliff and the other defended by massive terraces and zigzag walls. The invading Spanish were excellent castle-builders. They were awestruck by Sacsahuaman's size and fortifications. The Incas regarded warfare as an extension of religious ritual. Sacsahuaman was certainly used for religious ceremonies. Some historians claim that the Inca capital was laid out in the shape of a giant puma, with Sacsahuaman as its head.

SIEGE WARFARE

An Inca army takes on the enemy at Pukara, near Lake Titicaca. Most South American cities were walled and well defended. Siege warfare was common. The attackers blocked the defenders' ways of escape from the town. After the conquest, in 1536, Inca rebels under Manko Inka trapped Spanish troops in Cuzco and besieged them for over a year.

Inca helmets were round in shape and made of wood or cane. They were decorated with braids and crests.

4 Measure and cut a 3cm/1¼in yellow felt square, a yellow circle with a diameter of 3cm/1¼in, a 9cm/3½in yellow square and a 5.5cm/2¼in black square.

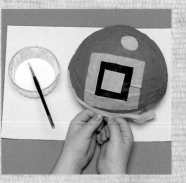

5 Glue the felt shapes on to the helmet as shown above. Glue a 2cm/¾in-wide strip of yellow felt along the edge of the helmet to neaten the edge.

6 Take 12 strands of black wool, each 30cm/12in long. Divide them into three hanks of four strands. Knot the ends together, then braid to the end.

7 Knot the end of the finished braid. Make two more. Glue them inside the back of the helmet. Wait until it is dry before trying it on.

Eclipse of the Sun

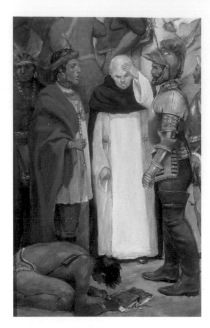

IN NOVEMBER 1532, the emperor Ataw Wallpa met the Spanish invaders, under Francisco Pizarro, in the great square of Cajamarca. The *Sapa Inca* was riding in a litter that was covered in feathers. Surrounding him were troops glinting with gold. The sound of conch trumpets and flutes echoed around the buildings. The Spanish were amazed by the sight, and the Incas looked uneasily at the strangers with their fidgeting horses.

Within just one hour, thousands of Incas had been killed, and their emperor was in the hands of the Spanish. Ataw Wallpa was arrested. He offered to raise a ransom to secure his release. Silver and gold arrived by the ton, filling up a whole room. The Spanish gained unimagined riches. Even so, in the summer of 1533 they accused Ataw Wallpa of treason, and he was garrotted (executed by strangulation). Resistance to the Spanish continued for another 39 years, but South American civilization had changed for ever that day.

THE WORD OF GOD?
When emperor Ataw Wallpa met the Spanish invaders in Cajamarca, he was approached by a Christian priest called Vincente de Valverde. The priest raised a Bible and said that it contained the words of God. Ataw Wallpa grabbed the book and listened to it. No words came out, so he hurled it to the ground. The Spanish were enraged, and the invasion began.

CONQUEST AND SLAVERY
The Spanish conquest was a disaster for all the native peoples of the Americas. Many of them were murdered, enslaved or worked to death in the mines. The Spanish introduced money into Inca life, trading in silver, gold, farm produce and coca. But it was mostly the Spanish settlers who became wealthy, not the native people.

"SANTIAGO!"
Before the 1532 meeting with Ataw Wallpa in the great square of Cajamarca, the Spanish invader Francisco Pizarro had hidden troops behind buildings. When he shouted the pre-arranged signal of *"Santiago!"* (St James), they began to shoot into the crowd. Chaos broke out as the emperor was seized and taken prisoner.

TEARS OF THE MOON

In 1545, the Spanish discovered silver at Potosí in the Bolivian Andes and began to dig mines. The wealth was incredible, but the working conditions were hellish. Local people were forced to work as slaves. Mule trains carried the silver northwards to Colombian ports, making Spain the richest country in the world.

DESCENDANTS OF THE EMPIRE

Christians of Quechuan and mixed descent take part in a procession through Cuzco. In the Andes, over the past few hundred years, many Inca traditions, festivals and pilgrimages have become mixed up with Christian ones. Indigenous peoples today make up 45 per cent of the total population in Peru, 55 per cent in Bolivia, and 25 per cent in Ecuador.

THE TREASURE FLEETS

The Spanish plundered the treasure of the Incas and the minerals of the Andes. Big sailing ships called galleons carried the gold and silver back to Europe from ports in Central and South America. The region was known as the Spanish Main. Rival European ships, many of them pirates from England, France and the Netherlands, began to prey on the Spanish fleets. This led to long years of warfare. Between 1820 and 1824, Spain's South American colonies finally broke away from European rule to become independent countries, but most of the region's native peoples remained poor and powerless.

Glossary

A

akllakuna Girls selected for special education and training in the Inca capital.

alloy Any metal made from a mixture of other metals.

alpaca A llama-like animal, valued for its wool.

aqueduct A channel carrying water supplies. It may take the form of a bridge when it crosses a valley.

archaeology The study of ancient remains and ruins.

ashlar A squared-off block of stone, used for building.

astrology The belief that the stars, planets and Moon influence the way we live on Earth.

astronomy The observation and scientific study of the stars, planets and other heavenly bodies.

ayllu A land-holding clan, made up of people descended from the same ancestor.

B

backstrap loom A system of weaving in which the upright (warp) threads are stretched between a post and a belt around the weaver's waist.

barracks Buildings used to house soldiers.

barter To exchange one item for another, to swap. This is the way in which goods may be acquired in societies that have no money.

blood-letting Cutting a patient to lose blood, for medical reasons.

bola Three heavy balls tied to cords. It was used by soldiers as a weapon and by hunters and herders to bring down birds and running animals.

bronze A metal alloy, made by mixing copper with tin.

C

cassava A starchy root crop, first grown for food in the Americas. It is also called manioc.

chicha Strong beer made from fermented maize.

chullpa A burial chamber in the form of a tower.

coca A South American plant whose leaves were used by the Incas as a mild drug, as a medicine and for fortune-telling.

compound An enclosed yard surrounding a building or group of buildings.

conch A large seashell that makes a booming sound when it is blown.

conscription A term of service to the State, in which people have to fulfil duties as workers or soldiers.

D

distaff A cleft stick used to dispense thread for spinning.

drill A length of wood that is rotated rapidly against another. The friction makes it so hot that it can be used to start a fire.

drop-spindle A hand-held weight used to draw out thread and spin it into yarn.

E

empire A group of lands ruled or governed by a single country.

G

gables The pointed ends of a house, supporting the roof.

garrison A force of soldiers posted to guard a fortress or a town.

gourd A hard-skinned fruit, often hollowed out for use as a container.

guanaco A wild relative of the llama, commonly hunted.

I

incense A gum or any other material that is burned to produce sweet-smelling smoke during religious ceremonies.

indigenous Originating from a country, native.

irrigation Bringing water to dry lands so that crops can be grown.

K

kero A drinking vessel.

kuraka One of the local chiefs of lands conquered by the Incas.

L

litter A chair or platform in which someone is carried.

llama A camel-like creature of South America. It is used as a pack animal, shorn for its wool and was sacrificed in religious ceremonies by the Incas.

loom A piece of equipment used to weave cloth.

M

mamakuna Virgins of the Sun, selected from the *akllakuna* to remain unmarried and lead religious lives.

manioc A starchy root crop, first grown for food in the Americas. It is also called cassava.

mit'a Conscripted work, owed to the Inca state as a form of tax.

mummy A dead body preserved by being dried out in the sun, by extreme cold or by using mixtures of chemicals.

N

niche A hollow inset in a wall.

nobles People high in social rank.

O

omen A sign of good or bad fortune in the future.

oracle A mysterious telling of one's fortune, or a shrine.

overseer A supervisor or boss.

P

panaka A land-holding corporation made up of nobles who were related to each other.

panpipes A series of pipes, normally of cane, joined to make a single musical instrument. Sounds are produced by blowing over the open ends.

pendant A piece of jewellery that hangs down, usually from the neck.

plateau Geographical feature of high, flat land, usually among mountains.

plumbline A weighted cord, held up to see if a wall or other construction is vertical.

pyramid A large monument with a square base, rising to a point or with steps up to a platform.

Q

quinua A plant whose seeds can be used to make a sort of porridge and whose leaves can be cooked like spinach.

quipu A series of knotted, dyed cords used to record information.

Quya The Inca empress, who was the sister-wife or mother of the emperor.

S

sacrifice Ritual killing of people or animals to please the gods.

Sapa Inca One of the titles taken by some Inca emperors, meaning 'Only Leader'.

sling A length of cord used to hurl stones or other missiles.

smelt To heat rock to a high temperature, melting and extracting the metal that is contained within it.

squash A type of vegetable commonly eaten by the Incas.

T

textile Cloth produced by weaving threads together.

topos A unit of measurement used in the Inca Empire, equal to about 7km/4 miles.

trapezoid Having four sides, of which only two are parallel. The Incas often used trapezoid shapes when designing windows and doors.

trepan Boring a hole in someone's skull for medical or religious reasons.

tribute Taxes paid in goods by conquered people.

tumi A ceremonial knife with a semi-circular blade.

tupu A long pin used by women to fasten clothing together. The Incas did not have buttons.

V

vicuña A llama-like animal whose wool was used to make the finest cloth.

W

wa'qa A shrine, a holy place or holy object.

Index